PATHWAYS TO POSSIBILITY

Also by Rosamund Stone Zander

The Art of Possibility
with Benjamin Zander

Pathways

TO

Possibility

Transforming Our Relationship with
Ourselves, Each Other, and the World

Rosamund
Stone
Zander

VIKING

VIKING

An imprint of Penguin Random House LLC
375 Hudson Street
New York, New York 10014
penguin.com

ISBN 9780670025183
Ebook ISBN 9780698195547

Printed in the United States of America
1   3   5   7   9   10   8   6   4   2

Set in Electra LT Std
Designed by Cassandra Garruzzo

While the author has made every effort to provide accurate telephone numbers, Internet addresses, and other contact information at the time of publication, neither the publisher nor the author assumes any responsibility for errors or for changes that occur after publication. Further, the publisher does not have any control over and does not assume any responsibility for author or third-party Web sites or their content

To my grandchildren and their future

Contents

PATHWAYS TO POSSIBILITY

Intro

duction

If you do not change direction, you may end up where you are heading.

LAO TZU

IN THE DECADE AND a half since the publication of *The Art of Possibility*, its ideas and stories have evolved into something like a movement. People from multiple walks of life have taken up the practices and embedded them in their workplaces or in their family life. We get letters of gratitude from many with whom we have no connection—the producer who attributes the existence of the wonderful film *As It Is in Heaven* to reading *The Art Of Possibility*, a candidate for public office who whispers that he keeps it by his bedside as his guide. A company that was the only one in its industry that went cash positive in the 2007–9 downturn attributes its success to the concepts and messages in *The Art of Possibility*. We received a newspaper article in the mail that informed us that President Uribe of Colombia offered the book as his only gift to President Chávez of Venezuela in tense times, and we heard from many a parent grateful for being able to get on a more life-enhancing track with a son or daughter.

We cast out a pebble in a pond, and we are unable to see the extent of the ripples although we know they go far. In those inter-vening years, Ben and I, the authors of *The Art of Possibility*, haven't stood still. Nor has the earth, for that matter. It has spun through some sixty-three billion miles of space in the interim, sweeping up new information from the universe and sending out its own mes-sages. Meanwhile, Ben's activities have accelerated, as he has pre-sented our model of Possibility to groups and institutions on every continent. His astounding energy seems to gather its resonance from the world around him, like fine crystal emitting harmonics at the touch of a finger.

While Ben has been circling the globe, I have been doing a deep dive into the inner world of our being, on a mission to discover how we may continue to grow beyond what we settle for as maturity. Most of us associate "growing up" with reaching a certain age, or taking on responsibilities, or passing our wisdom and resources on to the next generations. But I believe that when we become aware of patterns in our behavior, when we learn to identify and rewrite the stories that give us our identities, we will gain passage, at any age, into a new phase of adulthood. In this territory of maturity, where old fear-based patterns no longer hold us back, we will, I wager, do what we now think of as remarkable, even magical, things. In defiance of the adage "You Can't Change People," people around us will change in our presence, step into productivity and contribu-tion, and flourish. In this further phase of adulthood, we might well be agents for powerful action in the collective interest, helping rain forests to renew themselves, children to dedicate themselves to worthwhile pursuits, and relationships between nations to thrive. And further, when we become aware and adept at putting our out-dated stories out of their misery and creating new ones, we have a pretty good chance of experiencing that sense of profound and ec-static connection to the universe that monks and shamans talk about. It's to understanding and articulating this vision of human growth and expansion that I have dedicated the last fifteen years.

The mission of *The Art of Possibility* was to teach people to dis-tinguish two broad categories of approaches to life: one is the everyday attitude we call the "downward spiral," with all its joys and sorrows, triumphs and losses. The second approach we named "radiating possibility," and it is the attitude that life is a story we tell and live. The underlying assumption of the downward spiral is that life is all about survival, where you stand to win big if you are clever enough, get the right education, meet the right people, and make the best choices. But of course, chance and circumstances being what they are, in the downward spiral you are always faced with the fearful prospect that you might also lose. Your money may run out, the power you once enjoyed may disappear overnight, and the love you counted on may wane, or indeed be snatched away.

In the second approach, "radiating possibility," you can change your story at any time to be better adapted to the magnificent flow of the way things are, and the world will reflect the change in you, opening doors and showing you a path to where you want to go and what you want to do. This outlook gives rise to joy, love, and gratitude, leaving room for fear only in circumstances where feeling fear will mobilize you best to avoid an immediate threat to life and limb—a truck bearing down on you, for instance; not the prospect of losing someone's affection or being fired from your job.

So the first outlook, the downward spiral, is about the struggles over winning and losing, and the second, radiating possibility, is about creating the world in which you want to live. Each one is accompanied by its own distinctive postures, emotions, and expression. Each is a way of *being*. If, after spending time with *The Art of Possibility*, people were able to distinguish between the two attitudes through doing the practices, Ben and I felt we had accomplished our mission. At that point readers had a choice of perspective, and as a rule they chose to live in Possibility.

The current book, *Pathways to Possibility*, is firmly situated in the realm of possibility, but its mission is not focused on the distinction between the two attitudes addressed above. Your experience may deepen if you have read or choose to read *The Art of Possibility*, but it is not a necessary starting point for your journey through this manuscript. The mission of this book is to illuminate new pathways for growth. Throughout history, we human beings have bumped up against glass ceilings that have stopped us in our tracks and prevented us from going any farther, even in our imaginations. And then come the breakthroughs. Someone beats the record of the four-minute mile, and the door swings wide open for others. A black woman refuses to go to the back of the bus, and the whole of America wakes up, cheering or fighting, and from then on everything is different.

The glass ceiling I am addressing in this book is related to our assumptions of our limits as to how much we can grow and change, whether we can change others and even affect the world at large, and how much freedom and joy we can experience. To begin dismantling these assumptions, I trace how patterns we blindly enact get started and what we can do to initiate new ones, so that as we grow fearlessly and shatter the glass ceiling holding us down, others around us will grow as well.

The first part of the book attempts to demonstrate how the inevitable traumas of childhood provoke the young person into rigid patterns of thought and behavior that persist into the future. These childhood lessons such as "don't show when you are upset" or "dogs (all) bite" are designed to help us feel safe, but may be a poor fit, and may actually provoke danger, when carried into adult life. An example would be an instance where a friendly dog approaches a person who believes dogs bite. The man brandishes a stick, and soon there may be two frightened beings on the attack. The different stories in this section show how patterns develop and how they can be reengineered to reflect life as it is now and ourselves as we are now, in contrast to the environment in which they were first conceived, and our minds as we first conceived them.

The second part of the book turns our attention outward, and expands our vision to enable us to see through the individual stories and patterns that hold *other* people back. We learn to generate the combination of energy and love that is likely to enhance the possibility we see in others. Having rewritten our own stories in an adult voice, we avoid the common trap of being advice givers (at best) and meddlers (at worst) and we become natural agents for *their* transformation. We learn to connect with others on an energetic level that creates a synergy for realizing our collective dreams.

The third part shows how, having gained the capacity to witness our own patterns and contribute to an environment in which others can grow, we can become pioneers of a new territory where world and mind, mind and world are one. In this section you will read stories of remarkable accomplishments by people who sought to move in tune with the way things are, clear of wishful thinking and ideology, their minds open to patterns laced throughout our world; people who have gained a perspective on their place in it that allows them to enter into energetic connection with life around them.

The final section of the book presents a series of "games" that will usher the reader into this new territory of possibility and connection. These belong to the category author/philosopher James Carse dubbed "infinite games," open-ended engagements with no winners or losers; games that offer only the joyousness of play. The promise of this section is great: if we engage fully, we are likely to discover facets of reality we have never before experienced, and become occasional conduits for rare moments of perfect attunement with life.

You might think, from reading this introduction, that the book falls into neat compartments, but it isn't so. It develops in the way life evolves, in a radiating, spiral pattern that is anything but linear. So you will find you are experiencing echoes of earlier stories and ideas throughout the progress of the narrative, and this structure may help to give you a deeper perspective on each concept as it recurs in a different form. The possibility is that you will undergo an evolution of sorts, like a creature moving from the ocean onto land, that will leave you more aware of your primal beginnings but with greater capacities to move effectively in a new and expanded territory of life.

PART I

THE
All of You,

in Stories

You come into the world as a unique expression of a pattern already in play. From here you begin to improvise meaning that folds into stories that form your behavior and become your reality, all so you have the best chance to feel safe and grow.

Part I shows us how these stories evolve and new patterns come into being along the way. It shows us how to assess them and how to go about changing them when they no longer support us, so that we can move competently into life as it is now with our hearts and minds fully integrated.

CHAPTER ONE

Voices, Ages, and Parts

I WORK BEST IN SILENCE in the wild. So I often write late into the fall on an island retreat, in Maine, when most visitors have already left to go back to the city. One particular day in October I walked down to the water and was looking out at the cove through a delicate screen of spruce branches. Lovely as the scene was— white sunlight on the water and all—I felt an unforeseen and quite unwelcome melancholy that sent my mind in three directions. One was to plan my escape from this troublesome sadness by leaving the island altogether and rejoining the busy world; I certainly couldn't be faulted for that; the season was well past. Another was to fret over the failings of my day, as in, "What have I actually accomplished?" And yet at the same time, I was noticing how lucky I was to be in this beautiful landscape. The emotional incongruity was not new to me, but this time it jolted me awake. Those melancholic feelings had belonged to my *mother*, I suddenly realized. They were only barely my own!

I remember, as a child, my mother speaking of bleak or gloomy feelings particularly in the summer, and such talk unsettled me. As I was her chosen confidante, I was the likely candidate to hear stories of the experiences that had disturbed her. Maine had been the place where her family gathered after a winter apart, but it was also an environment where she felt most keenly rejected by her older siblings. Later, when my grandmother died, my mother and her siblings had argued over the disposition of a family house that stood high above Penobscot Bay. As they were unable to agree, it was eventually sold—to my mother's regret. All of the members of that generation settled into summer houses of their own, but the tension between my mother and one of her sisters continued as an undercurrent whenever they were both in residence in that small community, until her sister passed away. Although Maine had meant privacy to my mother—a place of beauty and relaxation where she felt protected from the pressures of society—she wouldn't walk alone in the spruce woods for fear of the dark.

So even as I felt those twinges of sadness, I realized that while for my *mother* there were many disheartening memories associated with the trees and water, that was not true for me. I love the woods; I lived in a tent in the forest by the ocean for an entire summer by myself and was pretty much in ecstasy. So I surmised—as I stood there looking through the screen of dark spruces at the white sparkling water—that *something*, the slant of sunlight perhaps, or the sound of the bell buoy in the distance, put me in touch with a six- or seven-year-old part of myself that had absorbed my mother's feelings and her history. At that thought, a smile came over my face, the wisps of melancholy dispersed, and the landscape became once again the place I wholeheartedly enjoy. It occurred to me that in that little transformative awareness, I had redeemed us both, for notwithstanding moments of unhappiness, my mother had been inspirational in her love of the coastline, and that, too, had rubbed off on me.

"All of us, when we engage in relatedness, fall under the gravitational influence of another's emotional world, at the same time that we are bending his emotional mind with ours." I was struck by this passage in *A General Theory of Love,* by three neuroscientists, and had mused over what is really happening as we bring up our children, or share experiences with colleagues or friends. Are our minds covertly drawing their minds into attunement? Are theirs drawing ours?

Now looking out over the water, I asked myself, how is it possible that I can say "I feel sad" and a moment later I say, "No, it is not I that feels sad, but only a part of me that has absorbed my mother's sadness"? To what am I referring when I use the word "I"?

EMOTIONAL MASTERY: PART ONE

To shed some light on these questions and gain some mastery in the emotional arena, let's imagine for a moment that you and I comprise many different voices, ages, and identities. Picture that below your consciousness a host of characters have been busy making themselves comfortable in your psyche, like mice in the basement, heedless of how their presence fits with any business you are trying to conduct. Or imagine that these characters are like a family of invisible children that troop along with you to your employer's house for lunch, and just as you are making an important point, one of them upsets his water glass, or decides your boss is taking advantage of you and derails the deal.

And all the while you, like everyone else, take pride in being the master of your destiny. (The inner kids are having a good chuckle at that one.) Almost everyone, when confronted with some unpleasant piece of behavior he has performed that disturbs his sense of control, finds a way of justifying it, often by foisting the blame somewhere else.

"If you were more committed to me I wouldn't be so sullen."

"Sorry I haven't called—I've been deluged with work."

Sometimes those inner folks seem to be completely at odds with one another, as when with the best intentions to follow a course of discipline—a diet, say, or exercise regimen—you indulge. Or, you come dazzlingly close to someone and then you just disappear. Huh?

The best explanation for all this is that some parts of you, parts with the self-doubt or combativeness of a teenager, or even the confusion of a very young child, step forward and hijack the show. Then, predictably, they do it again, forming a pattern as distinctive as water in a riverbed.

Let's say that in frustration you complain to your friends, not for the first time, that a certain person is late for dinner, or doesn't call when he swore he would. They sigh and shake their heads over your inability to see the obvious: "That's just the way he is," they say. "You won't change him." No, that's not who he is, it's just one of his characters who keeps stepping up. But if you find yourself hoping that he won't do it again, well, that hope resides in a part of you, age five or seven or nine, who was impelled to trust someone who was patently unreliable, for your own survival's sake. That part of him and that part of you have minds of their own—they are not under his or your conscious control—and given certain circumstances, are bound like clockwork to come to the fore.

Each "part" of us appears to have a point of view about how life should go and is living a story of its own. Some of the stories grow out of the rubble of a traumatic situation where, as children, we perceive a life-threatening danger and figure out what to do about it. The story and patterns initiated in these instances we will call "safety patterns."

Other stories may get their impetus from the necessity to distinguish oneself in the sibling group, to get enough attention from the parents. It almost never happens that two children born consecutively into a family pop up with the same personality and identical interests. Each seems to know intuitively that he cannot bask in the very spot in the sunlight of parental attention that his sibling occupies and develops a unique way of being: what we call personality.

Personality is a major story for human beings, a narrative that gets defined and polished as time goes on.

Finally, some of our stories are shaped through daily exposure to the surrounding culture, beginning with the family. It's the story a person is "living into" that we notice when we identify someone as of a certain class, or as liberal or conservative, or as hailing from a certain country, or perhaps as our type or not our type. Our own stories are mixed in there as well, of course.

In the ensuing chapters you will see, through personal accounts, how individual stories are acquired and transformed. You will begin to understand how to find and articulate the physical, emotional, and cognitive patterns that are currently governing you, and you will learn to see them from the perspective of their author, yourself at a younger age, so that you will be able to rewrite them.

We begin our voyage with a trauma-based story in which we witness how a safety pattern was born out of a series of interactions that created fear in a child and overwhelmed his capacities. You may not always find this young hero of ours sympathetic, and that's intentional—desirable even. I want you to stay at an interested and neutral distance from which you can view Alan as he grows and perhaps find some aspects of yourself in him to consider with the same dispassion. My intention is to help to strengthen the observing part of you that really is your most valuable tool for making any changes.

So we open with the tale of this young boy, Alan, a child of divorce, who remembers the excitement of his father arriving from afar on Christmas Eve when he was three and a half.

CHAPTER TWO

Alan's World

A MAN IS RETURNING AS a visitor to his former home carrying Christmas presents for his two children: for his five-year-old daughter he bought a large stuffed panda bear and for his three-year-old son a gift of a windup music box made of glass. We might debate the appropriateness of such a gift for a three-year-old boy, but no one would deny that such an unusual item might seem magical to a child. However, just before he received the wondrous glass box into which you could look and see tiny tines plinking against a moving cylinder, little Alan Spingold's mother whispered that she had a secret to tell him. She leaned over and spoke these subversive words, softly in his ear: "You're not going to like Daddy's present, but I'll make it up to you. I'm going to give you a stuffed bear just like the one he is giving to your sister."

This frightening message was much too complicated for the child to process. On Christmas Day, when he opened his presents, he discovered he loved the music box he wasn't supposed to love; and he also loved the bear his mother gave him. Feeling upset and exposed, he yearned for relief. What could he do to feel secure? His young mind did not have the capacity to imagine that this wasn't about him. There was no way that he could conceive of the idea that his parents might be acting out ancient, multigenerational problems of clandestine affiliations and betrayal.

Lying awake that night, the big stuffed bear by his side, and the glass music box concealed under the covers, Alan listened, troubled, to the voices arguing in the living room below. Then a brilliant solution found its way into his three-year-old mind and heart. His ancestors murmured approval from the dark corners of his room. Aha! If he kept his loves a secret, he could have them both, a bear and a music box, a mother *and* a father.

Now in his fifty-sixth year, Mr. Alan Spingold hasn't made any connection between his overt memory of that Christmas long ago and his deep-rooted pattern of infidelity. His dalliances had always seemed so logical—and of little importance. He told himself that his needs were unmet in his marriage; that not all men are designed to be monogamous; that in sophisticated circles, taking a mistress is quite common. . . .

His close friends, in discussing him, often shook their heads. "It would be dignifying his behavior to call it 'teenage,'" they said. "He is acting like an emotional three-year-old!" And indeed he was.

As thinking creatures, we don't tolerate well the illogic of our emotion-based impulses, so our minds will always produce reasons for the things we do, even when there is no connection whatsoever between our actions and what we say about them. Alan's mind produced rationales to fill in the blanks between a three-year-old's fear and an adult's impulses. On a visceral level, his fear-driven instinct told him that if he hid his love for each warring parent from the other, neither would leave him. That strategy for keeping himself safe created links and neuronal pathways that would remain active for years to come. Later on, whenever he felt the slightest disapproval from a woman with whom he was intimate, his feet, seemingly on their own, would seek out another lover. Double-dealing in secret appeared as his only possible strategy to cope with a loved one's displeasure or a colleague's frown, the seeds of which were delivered along with his father's bewildering absences and his mother's fateful whisper.

Alan's story and the patterns of action it stimulated were formed implicitly, that is, quite outside of his awareness. Almost from birth, Alan's nervous system had been captivated by his mother's intimate ways and shaped by his father's tendency to attach elsewhere. His Christmas quandary was an outcome of their patterns colliding, and it prompted him to discover a way of moving forward for himself out of the material that lay at hand: episodic intimacy, abandonment, and betrayal. It was the air he breathed.

Alan's life unfolded and proliferated under the banner of "Love in Secret," like a tree putting out branches, each new move a variation of the last. He formed multiple close relationships to anchor his fragile sense of attachment, like a toddler who moves from table to chair, never letting go of the furniture. During his school days, he had unusual friendships with teachers and mentors, and uncommonly close ties with the parents of his friends. In college when he dated he always had more than one girl on a string, though each of the young women felt comfortable that she was the favorite. Obtaining a degree in law, he gravitated toward opening a private law practice where he found himself engaged in one privileged conversation after another. Not long after he was married, he started to have affairs, but he was so discreet and so genuinely interested in treating each relationship with "integrity" (or so he told himself) that there was hardly ever any disturbance. . . .

GENERATIONAL PATTERNS

Patterns of this sort are generally not stand-alones. We could say that Alan's life was an offshoot, an altered copy of his parents' lives, and theirs, on deeper investigation, were iterations of their parents'. Alan's mother, Sarah, lost her beloved father in childhood, and subsequently lost her mother's attention as she became immersed in grief. Alan's father, Lou, was an only child of divorced parents, like Alan. Alan's grandmother had whisked Lou away from any contact with his own father, and Lou unintentionally perpetuated the pattern with his son. Lou found himself in multiple relationships of a secret nature, though of course Alan "knew" nothing of these facts when his three-year-old self came up with his brilliant strategy for remaining in connection with his separated parents.

How can it be that patterns so reliably repeat through generations, yet so often catch us unawares? We know how family traditions are *overtly* handed down: through the lighting of candles and reading of scriptures, through shared credos and family stories. Parents take children to art museums and talk of values and insist that kids come to the dinner table to eat together and discuss world affairs; or perhaps they keep a pot simmering on the stove for impromptu meals, should neighbors drop in. As children grow into adults, they often talk about these memories and discuss how they have used or discarded these traditions in their own lives.

Patterns of life that are explicit are easy to follow, modify, or reject, but not so with patterns that travel underground in subterranean rivers below our awareness. What are the mechanisms by which implicit emotional "traditions" and patterns of action are transmitted?

The answer is remarkably simple: they just rub off on you. We learn the ways of others by being around them, without ever having to think about it. An infant wrapped in the blanket of his mother's or caretaker's style of relating learns the nuances, the gestures, the stops and starts of love without ever "understanding" what is happening or, as in learning to speak, ever becoming conscious of what he has learned. Love is for all time, then, made up of the particular dance steps he had with his mother and she with others. If she is well and secure, he will learn that love is something akin to generosity, loyalty, and joy. If she is troubled, he will learn the lessons of her troubled relationships, that "love" is perhaps entrapping and frightening or explosive or demeaning.

PATTERNS IN THE SPINGOLD FAMILY

We would have to go back generations in the Spingold family to see all the patterns at work. But from the glimpse we have, we can surmise that Alan's parents, Lou and Sarah, were having some difficulty before Alan was born. Perhaps the pregnancy and the anticipation of becoming a father for a second time stirred up in Lou some disturbing memories of the disruption of his original family. Judging from his later behavior we could posit that he found himself going to another woman for comfort. As we play out our story, we might imagine that Lou's absence would bring up in Sarah old feelings of hurt over her father's death, subjecting the baby in her womb to a wash of sadness conveyed from mother to child through the changing rhythms of her heartbeat and the tightening of her muscles. The feel-good chemical oxytocin, which a mother's body produces at birth and with breast-feeding, may well have been in short supply for both mother and child under Sarah's emotional stress. So in this scenario, the infant Alan would likely have emerged into the world braced for danger.

Now let's say his mother, Sarah, wasn't able to tune in well to her baby's needs, her capacities overwhelmed by her emotional turmoil over the absence of the two important men in her life, her straying husband and the father she mourned for. Alan himself may not have been able to relax in her arms, either because of the atmosphere of tension or because she wanted more response from him than he knew how to give. One can certainly imagine that Sarah would have reacted negatively to anything less than a wholly accepting attitude from her infant.

So as in a choppy sea, where competing waves intersect and create interference patterns, the themes of loss and resistance to entrapment traveling through the generations made up the crosscurrents of Alan's world. By the Christmas of his fourth year Alan was probably as familiar with this particular emotional weather as a child of sailors is accustomed to the power of the wind and the rocking of the boat.

We know that Alan was struggling as a toddler to connect safely with each of his parents, in a discordant environment of intermittent intense intimacy from his mother, and random contact with his father. Psychologists have turned their attention to naming those earliest attachment patterns because of the influence they have on a child's ability to flourish.

ATTACHMENT PATTERNS

When the caretaking parent is able to attune to her infant and respond appropriately to his needs over time, she could be said to be providing an atmosphere of "secure attachment." Barring other influences, the child is likely to grow into an adult who, without anxiety, is able to balance independence and dependence and express feelings openly. However, if the child is brought up in an environment where the caretakers are sporadically more in tune with their own memories and troubles than they are with their baby, as were perhaps both Spingold parents, their child is likely to experience the effects of "ambivalent," or "anxious," attachment. He may learn that people are not dependable, feel anxiety over separation, and have difficulty reading feelings. Another pattern psychologists name is the "avoidant" attachment style, where the atmosphere in the home is one of consistent emotional distance and neglect. The product of such an upbringing is likely to view the world as a cold place where he has no chance to make an impact, and later may say, "I don't ever remember being hugged; in fact I remember very little of my childhood." And finally, if the parents' own concerns are overwhelming to them and incite them to unpredictable responses or violence, the pattern is called "disorganized." In this case the child is faced with the difficult task of integrating his need to come close to his parents and his need to escape the danger they present. His solution may be to become, in one way or another, emotionally absent as a result of his impossible dilemma.

Patterns Persist

Unwittingly, the parent who himself was never embraced and cherished may become frozen in a posture that gives insufficient comfort to his child. And children of divorce, alas, often find themselves at the brink of divorce no matter how determined they are to make great marriages. Children of tightly knit families may struggle for independence but often eventually find themselves holding on too tight. How an infant is drawn into relationship matters. Patterns of attachment that remain below consciousness tend to play out far into the future in novel iterations, like designs woven into handmade carpets, each, within its repeating rhythm, unique.

As an adult, Alan could not see the "repeat" in the patterns, as there was no precedent for self-examination in the environment in which he was raised. He simply didn't see the extent of the ambivalence and untrustworthiness that were pervasive in his relational life. He was not aware that all his connections were serving virtually the same purpose: hedges against anticipated loss, a loss that he had long ago experienced as a body sensation, and which was now simply a body memory. So, because the arrested child in him had had no guidance in growing up, fifty-two years later Alan was no better able to tolerate those memories of upset, fear, and exposure than he was when the circumstances overwhelmed him during the Christmas holiday at the age of three. His flight from those feelings had left him with a block on his heart that prevented him from growing and changing with a partner. He obviously could not reveal himself fully to any lover, or even to any friend. His own way of interpreting that was to characterize himself as a private person, but that was simply rationalization of what he sporadically knew to be true, that he was betraying people right and left. Now and again he would consider leading a straight life, but his relationships were so entangled that he couldn't conjure any way to do that. In any event, because each time he thought about it he saw nothing but loss, the idea scared the living daylights out of him.

Loss Arrives to Haunt Him

In his early fifties Alan became more captivated than usual with a particular woman he was seeing on the side. He prided himself on his ability to manage such complex situations. And then, at some point, it all fell apart. The very thing he had been staving off all his life, the eventuality that his friendly approach and his skills of listening and expertise at managing had been designed to prevent, happened. He was betrayed; he was abandoned. After twenty-five years of marriage, his wife, Betty, went off with another man. Soon thereafter the "other" woman, affronted by the depth of Alan's reaction to the disappearance of a wife whom he had all along characterized as "cold," and with whom he had claimed to have almost no relationship, vanished as well.

Alan spun into a state of shock and terror the likes of which he had never known before (he thought). He jumped at loud noises, he was overcome by waves of disbelief, punctuated by lurid images of *them* together; he couldn't eat or sleep. His mind wasn't able to grasp what was happening to him, but his body knew: it was reliving a memory of a time long before the three-year-old's escape into bifurcated loving. His body remembered the newborn's wail in the unresponsive dark.

As a jumble of lost feelings and memories rose up to hit him, Alan fell to pieces: his wife's "act of betrayal" forced its way past the defenses guarding those early emotional secrets and opened up circuitries of terror, fury, and helplessness that started firing at the sight of almost everything in his environment—a coffee cup, a sweater, signs of an unfinished project—anything that was remotely connected to her. Alan's mantra, "Love in Secret," had functioned as a giant resistance to the feelings surrounding the endangerment he experienced in infancy. Like so many of us who undergo crises, he hadn't a clue that what he had braced against all those years lived only in his memory. The baby had once been in mortal danger of losing his sense of connection to the living world, but the *memory* of that terror is not life threatening to the adult. Because Alan was unaware of the deeply grooved avoidance pattern he impulsively followed to save himself from reexperiencing that terror, he ended up like Oedipus, walking blindly into what became truly a major loss for his *adult* life.

CHAPTER THREE

Coming Apart

Insight into oneself is the same as calling yourself at home; the line is always occupied.

FROM THE MOVIE *THE SEA THAT THINKS*

THE MAJORITY OF US live in cultures where there is no tradition or any expectation of identifying patterns that affect us, or of tracing the unconscious ones that lead us where we have no intention of going. Competition, for instance, is a pattern that crops up in early childhood to help us get enough attention to support our growth, but then competition goes on embedding itself in adult life in areas where it does not belong. One has only to point out how competition dominates relationships with neighbors, business, and policies between states to remind one of the measure of its reach. How close are we to the brink of global collapse because industry can do nothing else but compete for market share and grow?

So Alan's hard fall appears to have been a blessing in disguise. It took a hit from a metaphorical two-by-four for him to become even remotely curious about the forces that were governing him. He had spent fifty years keeping the circuitries dormant that Betty's "infidelity" had suddenly hot-wired. That half century of sleep left the very impulses that were driving his behavior impermeable to change. The adage that trauma can herald a new beginning has merit, although it is too much to expect anyone feeling the shock to welcome such a thought. But it appears to be true; our nervous systems are most malleable when the pathways we want to change are activated.

But how was he to go about changing a pattern? In such cases, willpower, our usual standby to get things done, won't help. Will is useful for getting the garage cleared out, or tackling that pile of dirty dishes in the sink, or limiting your intake of chocolate. But surprisingly, your will is ineffective when trying to change patterns that are implicit, the kind that you adopted unknowingly from the environment in which you grew up. Your will won't be successful trying to alter the survival strategies that got you out of childhood alive or the reactions you have when your strategies fail. The patterns we are referring to are sourced from deeper structures in the brain, the limbic system and the reptilian complex, that are not under the control of the reasoning mind.

THE THREE-PART BRAIN

Our brains are often referred to as triune, divided into three parts, each initiated at a different stage in our evolution. The most ancient 500-million-year-old reptilian part is almost entirely reactive, moving faster than we can think, prompting us to flee or combat whatever appears to be dangerous, or freeze in the face of it. In these moments our frontal lobe, the seat of reason, flickers out, and we're on automatic pilot, instinctively moving into those primeval postures. It is into the fight/flight/freeze stance that trauma, and the memory of trauma, reliably send us.

The most recent part of our brain in evolutionary terms, the neocortex, often called the "thinking brain," began its expansion in primates barely two to three million years ago. It is this that allows us to analyze, investigate, and problem-solve; to distinguish, on a second glance, a root from a snake on the trail, or the words of a snake oil salesman from those of an honest purveyor. In the best case, our frontal lobe allows us to get some distance from what we feel and do. While the neocortex is clever in its ruminations, it is important to understand that, contrary to what you might expect, it does not lead our actions. It thinks, it predicts, it contrasts and compares, and it figures things out, all from its armchair. Instead, the emotional limbic system is the nominal commander in chief, and prompts us to do what we do.

The limbic system, which made its appearance about 150 million years ago with the advent of mammals and birds, is at the core of our brains. It is the emotional center that we share with all such sentient beings. Aided and abetted by our highly complex system of "mirror neurons" located in the motor portion of our brain that is responsible for the echoes of yawns, tears, and excitement we feel in witnessing one another in the throes of action, the limbic system offers up a wide range of experience from meaningfulness and connection to separation and loss. Our limbic brain is not simply reflexive, but induces us to love and fight with passion. Under the best of circumstances, it pairs with the neocortex to send us wisely on our way.

An optimum pairing of these two parts of the brain takes place when we accept this premise: that the life that to us seems real is but a stand-in for whatever may be out there, filtered through layers of perceptual twists and assumptions. And this, too: that our actions are drawn forth by that stand-in, that story we tell that we are convinced is real. When we thoroughly adhere to these propositions, our thinking brain is free to create new narratives that draw us away from the reflexive, fear-provoking images of the ancient reptilian brain and fortify the limbic system to move us where we best would go. Here is the beginning of the answer as to how we can change those implicit patterns that are not under our conscious control.

Before we explore that idea further, let's see what happened to Alan in his trauma, and how, over time, he was able to lead himself out of the morass.

CRACKS EVERYWHERE

When Alan broke down, he felt ruptures and splits throughout every part of him, mind, body, and soul. The first thing he wrestled with was finding a coherent story to explain what had happened. "Who is this stranger that I'm married to that she would do this? How was I such a fool not to see it coming?" were his first thoughts, alternating with "Where did I go wrong? How did this happen? What did I do?" The questions could not be answered because there were just too many parts of Alan in the act, each with its own age and point of view. The infant part of him that knew the terror of abandonment when answers to his cries were long delayed or never came, felt Betty's betrayal was proof that she wanted him dead and gone; the long-suffering child in him, who had waited so patiently for his father, thought, "She can't really have left, she will eventually come back to me"; the pseudo-adult—the part of him that wanted to seem grown up—yearned for a judge to prove him right; and the teenager was outraged at being "dissed" as a lover. Depending on which voice was in ascendancy, Alan labeled Betty this way or that. "She can't love" satisfied one. "She's trying to suppress her feelings for me," cried out another. "She'll be back, she's just running scared," called out another. The pseudo-adult proclaimed, "She's a narcissist. She would rather gratify herself than act with decency," while the teenage part asserted, "She's fantasizing about us having sex right now." Alan was in emotional pieces, unable to integrate the experience into any consistent story line. What description of this woman would explain everything, and why wasn't he tipped off sooner to the sort of woman she was?

There is, of course, no answer. Life is a story we tell, and the many parts of Alan were telling different stories. This was very distressing to him because his (and our) sense of wholeness depends on our achieving some kind of coherent narrative of our lives, and some kind of cooperation between the disparate parts. Before the betrayal, Alan's "lifestyle" had served to calm the fear of abandonment held by the infant part of him, as there was always another woman waiting for him in the wings. It meant also that the fatherless child did not have to anticipate any delay in connection. He had only to pick up the phone to make one. Alan had characterized his reactive need for an extra woman as "part of a cultural tradition," "the way I'm wired," and "nice work if you can get it" — a cohesive enough narrative to give him the sense that he was in charge, although it took energy to support such questionable statements. The problem was there was no allowance within it for Alan's relationships to grow, or for Alan himself to develop, because he was always in hiding—from himself as well as others. While Betty matured, he only aged, and over time he became less and less attuned to her.

But now, due to a deafening wake-up call that threatened forever to banish sleep, Alan was poised for change. Alan did indeed have a window open for transformation, as long as he regarded it thus. But change doesn't take place just by laying bare the circuitry; it happens in the way the pathways were originally built, in the milieu of emotional contact. New habits are formed in an environment of love.

CHAPTER FOUR

Adding a Part

ALAN'S COLLAPSE UNDER THE weight and chatter of his many internal voices prompted him to come for counseling. There was wisdom in this. He needed some kind of loving attention, and psychotherapy can often fill that bill. So after Alan had told me the high points of the drama, and after each of his parts had stepped forward with their needs and demands, and after I expressed my wonder at the cacophony of voices within him, I said, "Alan, I think you need yet *another* voice, *another* part that can oversee the sorting-out process. So bear with me. Let's try this.

"Imagine a wide 'field' stretching to the horizon," I continued. "We'll call it your 'field of awareness.' Picture it in your mind's eye as lush and fertile, with generative properties. Now post a sign in the ground with the name ALAN on it. This is not a field you own," I said. "This is who you *are*, a field named Alan. It includes every

aspect of you, who you have ever been and who you will become."
I promised him that if he is willing to think of and name himself
this way, as a field, he will have taken a first step toward assembling
the pieces into a well-balanced whole. He will no longer be identifying exclusively with any one of his clamoring parts. So when one
of them knocks that water glass over, he will not be the klutz, and
when the teenager in him preens around an attractive woman, he
will recognize his younger self, but he will not be mistaken that he
is that person with all its adolescent angst and pride. No, he is not
that part; he is the field in which all parts are arrayed.

His first assignment was to categorize troublesome feelings as
ancient memories — neural pathways laid down in his early history
that have become activated because of an association, a trigger. I
asked him to take it on faith that every feeling swirling around in
his heart and body was a memory. He wasn't to try to decide the
merits of framing emotions in this way, or whether it fit every case.
I asked him to regard his fury at the fact that his wife had left him
with an empty refrigerator as a memory of a feeling he had had
long before, and the writhing he felt in his body as he got into bed
as the same — a memory. I told him to name the shock he feels
when a strange woman looks alarmingly like his wife as a primor-
dial memory, and I told him to name the sickness in his stomach
and the sobbing all as memories.

I then asked Alan to get a feel for what part was crying out when
an emotion hit him. I told him it wasn't necessary to be accurate;
all that mattered was that he imagine himself as that younger person and try to get a sense of his age.

First, he just observed the children clamoring within and gave
them ages — for example, "This fear in the pit of my stomach feels
like a child who is lost; maybe he is four years old. The anger I am
experiencing now is the way I remember feeling in the tenth grade
when my teacher was unfair. This dark sense of despair seems as
though it is coming from a part of me that isn't able to speak yet."

The next step was to surround the internal children, when they
cried out, with compassion. Here is what he reported:

When I felt the fear in my gut, I tried thinking of myself as a baby, and I tried looking through his eyes. It was terrifying, like falling into a deep pit with no way out. I forced myself to say, although I didn't want to speak, "Oh, that's what it was like back then! How awful for that child." Actually, hearing my own voice made me less afraid, and it helped me to understand.

So then I tried to remember what it was like to be seven or eight waiting for my father, either on a weekend when he said he would come, or over the months when we didn't hear from him. I felt chronic hope and chronic disappointment like a disease with no cure, as though it were happening to me today. I stood next to the boy in my mind and put my arm around him. "I'm here now, kid, for good," I said, and held him tight.

When, in my mind, I came face-to-face with a younger part of myself who was trying to be grown up beyond his years, I was shocked. He was like a male prostitute who would do the bidding of anyone who would accept him on any level. It was appalling and extremely sad.

Putting on the shoes of the feisty, sexy teenager, I was surprised to realize how unimportant he felt, and I saw that he was thinking, "She wants the other man for something real and exciting." I got quite confused, actually, because the story seemed so accurate, but when I stood back and finally managed to view that as the adolescent part of me, I felt enormous compassion.

Then, from Alan's diary, came this transformational leap he shared with me:

On Thursday evening I had these thoughts, all very new. I noted that when babies feel abandoned, it is through no fault of their own. I also saw that boys who so heroically wait to connect with their fathers are a force of good in the world; and competent, responsible children who give themselves over lock-stock-and-barrel to the less able adults are really enormously generous, and must be treasured and respected as they learn to face their disappointments and let their dreams for a united family go. As for that energetic teenager, he was a pain in the ass, but thinking about him I found myself smiling with a parent's all-forgiving love.

As "Alan" grew into awareness, compassion flowed into isolated parts of him and his brain began to change, opening new connections, and bathing the fault lines with love. That's how it works. Your brain won't heal and change if you yell at it, or are impatient. That's like expecting a plant to flourish in the dark. A plant needs light and moisture and time to grow, and your brain needs attention and love.

Alan hardly recognized himself at this juncture. For six months he felt no temptation to go after women; he just didn't feel up to it. But when he started to make a contact (or two) he found that he was coming up against old patterns and old triggers in fast motion. When one woman distanced herself he felt frantic, even crazy, and waited in a high state of anxiety for the time when he would see her next. When he was with a lady who, unlike his parents, was more accommodating and attentive, he found to his embarrassment that his mind would wander, thinking about others.

Then one day it came to him: these women are memories; they are amalgams of my father and mother. A kind of elation hit him. In his mind's eye, he set about to strip memories of both rejection and entrapment from the women in his current life, like old wallpaper. He saw them as they were! Now Molly appeared to him not as smothering—just a little anxious and wanting to please. It hit him that Sonya wasn't snubbing him, she just preferred a little distance and it didn't mean anything about him! His biggest insight was that the highly fraught story of his distant, rejecting father had gotten stuck to the unsuspecting Sonya, and when he peeled it off in his imagination nothing was left but regard for her. After that, his first thought was "I should let her be." He might still have had a romantic interest in her, but he didn't. The impulse to get her attention was gone. Alan was flooded with affection for these women, but felt no need to go after them. The phobic block to his heart was melting.

It seemed truly miraculous to Alan that he could one moment experience a stab wound when a woman turned her back on him, and by a simple act of imagination heal the wound and step into a different reality. What power! He thought he could probably strike the set of any drama that gave him the old, familiar pain.

New Pathways Are Formed

A deeply embedded pattern had been rerouted in Alan's brain, his body, and his behavior toward others. But would it last forever? "Permanence" isn't the right vocabulary for these changes. The old pathways remain, gradually buried over time but still prone to activation in heavy weather. Yet each time Alan dropped into the ancient feeling of longing and rejection, he had a new opportunity to draw the curtain aside—mentally of course. He could choose to reflect on any incident as a memory, have that remarkable experience of seeing it from another angle, and thereby strengthen the new routes, those recently forged neural pathways. In time, he began to welcome the return of the old feelings because he began to see those moments as opportunities for more learning and change.

CHAPTER FIVE

Change

O VER A PERIOD OF three years, Alan "rewrote" many of the stories that had been setting the stage for his life so far. The key to the change was the authorial distance he achieved and maintained by naming himself as some kind of timeless field. From there he could look out from an infinite number of points of view, recognizing each as an aspect of himself; but about none of them did he say, "This is who I am." He saw all appearances as stories, so instead of thinking that "safety lies in having more than one intimate relationship" he saw the same data as "a story my three-year-old self made up to deal with the fears that were aroused by parents who couldn't get along." The story that he was "falling apart" changed to "I am experiencing many disconnected feeling states that are memories of events in the past."

Once he understood that the patterns he wanted to change

could be altered only with emotional energy, Alan adopted, one by one, a new set of explicit practices that he thought might open his emotional pores in restorative ways, and connect his head and heart. He took up the guitar—he had always wanted to—and when the weather warmed, he sat outdoors trying out chords and singing some romantic songs that had been popular in his youth. He found each moment deeply satisfying. He spent money on a great bicycle, and then a kayak, with the thought of immersing himself in nature. Once he went out to the middle of the bay near his house and sat for a long time, smiling in gratitude. He was no longer frantic, because there were no competing relationships that he felt he needed to secure. Slowly the tension of the anticipation of loss drained away. In its place, a sense of well-being arose, and with it a feeling of love for his surroundings, an opening of his heart.* He became present without urgency.

Alan came to understand, although he often couldn't hold on to the idea, that participating in sensual, expressive activities, like playing the guitar, which gave him so much pleasure, was exactly the path for him to follow so that he might love generously and well, and if he learned to do so, he would have no need to fear betrayal.

Over the three years of Alan's inward-facing work, his attention shifted day by day away from the urgency of maintaining a security guard of sexual partners to engaging in a broader, more loving relationship with people everywhere, and a warmer, more relaxed relationship with himself. He was delighted to find that women still turned his head exactly as they had before, but the impulse to

---

* In 1984, E. O. Wilson, the Harvard biologist famous for his work with ants, coined the term "biophilia" to denote what he claims is an innate craving in man for nature. In recent years a new discipline, ecopsychology, has gained traction, focusing on pathology arising from being out of touch with nature and designated in such terms as "nature deficit disorder," "eco-paralysis," and "eco-anxiety." See Daniel B. Smith, "Is There an Ecological Unconscious?," *The New York Times Magazine*, January 27, 2010.

connect with them, please them, and conquer them was slipping away.

Every once in a while Alan would take stock, and each time he did so he saw that he had moved a step farther away from the shock of his wife's leaving, but also from the traumas of his early life.

PRACTICES FROM ALAN'S WORLD

I see the story of Alan as a kind of Pilgrim's Progress, a journey of Everyman that transcends the particulars of his experience. Because his attachment to his troubled parents in early childhood was not secure, his existence, in more or less obvious ways, was all about trying to ensure his safety. He didn't realize his sense of danger was a memory and that there was nothing in his present circumstances to warrant it. Consequently, he found himself in a complicated series of attachments, lies, and subterfuges, all the while professing to be a man of integrity, and sometimes believing it. A major trauma disassembled the scaffolding of his life, and he found to his ultimate satisfaction that with the help of some practices he was able to rebuild it solidly from scratch, and get on with a far more fulfilling future.

Perhaps as a detached witness to Alan's growth, you were able to recognize, without judgment, parts of yourself in him. What follows is a description of the practices that enabled him to become free and grow, some of which will be expanded on later. You are welcome to try any or all of them, with or without a witness to your journey, but remember, habits are transformed in the presence of love.

PRACTICE NUMBER ONE: CALL YOURSELF
A FIELD OF AWARENESS

Name yourself as a field, a field of awareness. Just decide that's what you are, that's your story. As the field of awareness you have no opinions or plans, you are not for or against. You encompass everything past and present. You embrace all parts of yourself without bias, your hopes and all your mistakes; your memories and your talents, your skills and your pleasures, and all the pain you have ever experienced. As the field, your sight is clear, not blurred by the overlay of assumptions. You are consciousness itself.

Remember, the practice is simply to keep identifying yourself this way. It doesn't say anything about being successful at it.

PRACTICE NUMBER TWO:
NAME FEELINGS AS MEMORIES

Name curious or troublesome feelings and emotions as memories.

Emotions and memories arise in the same part of your brain and are closely linked; naming an unwanted emotion you are experiencing as a memory helps you to empathize with a younger version of yourself. The goal is to pair the feeling with the incident or age level to which it belongs. Then it becomes a memory of an event that you don't have to fix or escape, because it has already happened! If you stub your toe now, you know it's happening in the present, and you won't try to categorize the feeling as a memory— unless you are experiencing a fear around it that seems excessive.

So when you are having a disturbing feeling or a curious emotion, get a *feel* for the age of the memory—accuracy and specificity are not necessary. Then, if you think it is a memory of infancy, treat the baby in you as a baby, or if you feel for a moment like a teenager, regard that part of you appropriately for his/her stage of development.

Using your overseeing self, speak to your newly identified child parts with love and compassion. Wrap your arms around them.

PRACTICE NUMBER THREE:
PEEL YOUR MEMORIES OFF OTHERS

When a person (or people) in your present life trigger unwanted feelings in you, first view those feelings as memories and then intensify them. You will see that the story in which you have that person encased will probably have something to do with wanting approval or safety, or power, or desiring more closeness. It will be a story made up by a child. Peel those stories off like wallpaper in your mind, until you reveal the person in front of you as he truly is.

PRACTICE NUMBER FOUR: CREATE NEW NARRATIVES

From your position as the field, a certain kind of new narrative becomes easily accessible. "That was a story made up by a child" is one, or "That was a feeling I had as an infant."

In chapter 6 we will learn to create stories that specifically target those things that happen that feel so repetitive, like being cheated, perhaps, or choosing the wrong people to work with you, patterns from which it seems there is no escape.

PRACTICE NUMBER FIVE:
TAKE UP NEW EMOTIONAL HABITS

Sing, walk in nature, take up painting, play a musical instrument, join a yoga class, bicycle, or learn to create fancy pastries. Make the choice for stepping into life, rather than habitually numbing yourself with TV and video games. These active practices hold the possibility of connecting your mind, body, and emotions, enriching you with sensory data, building a sense of efficacy and power, and getting your blood flowing; all of which we know has a very positive effect on your mood. Along with your new identity and clarity, your improved relationship with parts of yourself and others, you may start to experience a profound connection with the whole world around you as you cycle down an avenue of trees or sing along with Maria Callas.

Practice Number Six: Overcome the Pull of Old Habits

To overcome the pull of old habits, stay mindful and surround yourself with people doing energetic things. Then raise your energy and radiate to the world. Sing! Laugh wildly! Clap extravagantly! Give long hugs. Express your gratitude and joy.

CHAPTER SIX

Running on Empty

Whereas Alan's pattern was to succumb to his need for attachment at the *expense* of the other relationships in his life, the young lady in the following story developed safety patterns that were by and large a *contribution* to others. Unlike Alan, whose task was to create a safe environment for himself out of two parties who had little positive connection between them, Sally's was to learn to thrive on minimal parental attention altogether. The clarity of the situation was an advantage for Sally. And luckily, she met her comeuppance, the failure of a major safety pattern, relatively early on in her development, affording her the prospect of a long life of growth and satisfaction.

We begin. Sally's birth did not mark a happy period in her mother's life. Throughout Sally's early childhood, her mother, Doris, told and retold the story of the long evening when she sat on the back stairs of their farmhouse in Connecticut, waiting anxiously for her husband to come home. Sally listened carefully and with fascination because she was featured in the story also, growing inside her mother. Through the umbilical cord she had received her share of the black coffee, chocolates, and cigarettes Doris consumed in her misery as she yearned for her husband to return. As Sally heard the story over and over, she came to the conclusion that it would have been a good trade had *she* disappeared and her father come back.

I say "she," but different parts of her absorbed different messages. One part was proud to be her mother's sounding board, one was willing to sacrifice herself for her mother's happiness, another experienced herself as competent, and one deep part "felt" that she should never have been born.

But as you may have gathered, Sally stayed and her father left. After Sally's birth, Doris took the baby to *her* mother's house where there were servants to help Doris recover from the surgery. Doris's mother — Sally's grandmother — was absent, as it was her custom to vacation in Europe in the spring.

It was common practice in those pre–Dr. Spock days, in families with means, to hire a baby nurse to give the infant a bottle on a strict four-hour schedule, mostly with little contact between feedings. The idea was to train the baby from the start to recognize who is boss. The theory was that if you let an infant cry long enough she would eventually stop, and over time cease crying altogether. The method was successful with thousands of babies: they did stop crying, but not before they had taken in implicitly, through many repetitions, that no one was out there to answer their cries, and that they themselves, in some primal sense, didn't matter. This practice was very different, of course, from that of a parent standing by, waiting alertly, while an infant learns to settle himself. In the latter case, an adult is there to sense how much separation an infant can manage that is positive, long before he goes into despair. Fortuitously, Dr. Spock came along and in respect for the children and their frantic or bewildered caretakers, preached a different wisdom, but the earlier childrearing philosophy, resistant as it was to change, may have been instrumental in creating a host of children affected by neglect trauma, who grew up unable to ask for what they needed, and became fanatically self-sufficient.

Sally heard the story from Doris that she cried like a crow, plaintively, from a distant room. A part of Sally thought, "How annoying of me." A preverbal part remembered the terror and the abyss.

Before Sally turned seven, Doris sent her off to overnight camp for two months—the same one Doris herself had attended as a child—and embarked on a long-held dream, a road trip to the far West. As for Sally, by the second week of camp she had caught a cold that gave her a few days' respite from the homesick, bedwetting society of her cabinmates, and promptly got a crush on the head nurse in the infirmary. Then, at the end of the fourth week she broke out with chicken pox and had to be quarantined in exile for an entire month. During this time Sally received but one giant postcard from her mother, with a full-color picture of the Grand Canyon in purplish evening light. She cherished every inch of it.

The last pox scab fell off a few days before the end of camp, and Sally was free to rejoin the group. She hit the ground running. She worked like a demon to win a set of shiny, intricately detailed archery, tennis, and swimming medals she had had her eye on from the first week of camp.

All the while, parts of Sally were writing instructions for her lifelong safety manual. "Hide your hunger for love and attention, stay strong and stay positive. Be sustained by a postcard." While designed to solve a chronic need for attention, these instructions hardly reflected a world eager to lend Sally a supportive hand.

Fortunately for Sally, Doris had the care and imagination to send her two daughters to a progressive primary school where Sally's creativity and self-esteem flourished. There she was allowed to engage in art projects as long as she wanted, and plunk down in an armchair to read as often as she wished. She formed a special relationship with almost every one of her teachers, as she had with the camp nurse. At home, she attuned herself closely to her volatile mother, assuring a series of random bonded moments, like crazy beads on a string. No matter what her mother did to her—love her, abuse her, forget about her—Sally popped right back up with excuses for her, and no matter that Sally did not hear from her father for years and years, she held on patiently to a secret hope that they would eventually be together. New instructions were added to the manual: be special, make excuses for others' failings, work hard to keep people around, never give up.

By the time she was eighteen and leaving for college, Sally had her act together. Her "act" was to shine in order to earn her place in others' hearts. She played the piano, won her high school writing prize, and starred on the debating team. She was a good listener and a recognized problem solver. She made herself indispensable in the service of avoiding a repetition of the trauma of early neglect, and with every challenge, she unconsciously revisited those postures—as in "stay strong" and "be sustained by a postcard"—that had brought her safety and relief, until all other potential paths faded and, for all practical purposes, disappeared.

Dry Farming

There is an upside to the work that goes into creating safety patterns in response to conditions of neglect. Just as grape vines, deprived of water by the knowledgeable farmer, send their roots down deep into the soil's substrata and emerge stronger and more self-sufficient from the process, so does the attachment-challenged child gain prodigious strengths of self-reliance and resilience when she has to work to get what she needs. If the conditions are too challenging, of course, or the vines find insufficient water, the young vine and the young child will fail to thrive.

Those skills a person gains by being left on her own to make it are likely to benefit her throughout her life. This is the theory behind the tradition of vision quests for Native American youths and wilderness programs for teens. It may also be the motive that drives parents to teach their children early on that the world isn't just theirs for the taking. However, the implicit safety patterns a person follows whose origins are not available to her conscious mind, like "hide your feelings" or "wait forever," are spanners in the wheel of life. Because they relate only to conditions in her past, and are therefore impervious to change with present circumstances, they are impediments to a person's progress to maturity.

Sally received enough nourishment to be proactive in extending roots. While other children were bargaining with their parents for all they could get, Sally was looking elsewhere for what she needed, which necessitated that she learn how to navigate a world where people had no obligation to her. She realized early on that relationships required something of her, and she delivered. She became precociously able to read people's feelings and situations, and it made her smart and strong and popular. Those skills were positive for her and the people around her and spurred her to grow toward adulthood.

Another part of her was driven by fear and sacrifice; despite all her privilege, that part was like a waif, savvy in the lore of the streets: "Stay alert! Remember, no one ever wanted you—you don't belong. Relax even for a moment and everything you have will disappear." These were visceral and emotional reactions stemming from conclusions she probably arrived at well before she could speak, and they were not positive; they drained her energy and stood in the way of her development.

What You Resist Persists

All survival strategies contain the shadow of a cataclysmic moment, the ghost of the past threatening to return. Many people meet that ghost somewhere along the road, and some escape the moment entirely; but not Sally. The comeuppance she had spent every ounce of energy staving off arrived unannounced when she was twenty-two. Her piano teacher, who had been a stable part of Sally's life for years, dropped her as a student, explaining that going forward he was keeping only those students who were making a professional career out of music. This should not have come as a great surprise because the man was getting up in years and it was logical that he should cut back on his teaching. But that had never crossed Sally's mind. In a repetition of her relationship to the red-headed nurse at camp, she had been utterly devoted to her piano instructor, working hard for him and bringing small gifts to her lesson—pastry and coffee (she knew how he liked it) or occasionally a book or an article she thought he would enjoy. If one could say she had been devoted to him beyond reason, she was now devastated beyond reason, and one more iteration of the old, multigenerational pattern played itself out.

The adage "what you resist persists" describes so much of our emotional life, and yet it is difficult to grasp the full meaning of the phrase, and why it should be so. One explanation is that when you are dedicated to avoiding emotions or experiences that once frightened you, you are less likely to see signs of what you dread coming toward you, in the way that Sally simply hadn't noticed that it was time for her beloved teacher to retire. It's the phenomenon of not seeing "the handwriting on the wall." You may rationalize away signs of illness or change, for instance, until they catch up with you and take you by surprise. Those safety instructions that were designed to protect you when you had little power to affect your circumstances now handicap the adult in you who has the ability to act on her own behalf.

Let's look at a more straightforward example. A fellow named Bob grows up as a middle child in a family rife with emotional turmoil, and he adopts the pattern of shutting it all out—going to his room to read, or simply turning his mind to other things. We would all understand that as a common-sense adaptation to his environment. Now Bob is a grown man, married to Alice, a calm and reasonable woman, the kind that his internal children initially adored because she posed no threat to them. However, there are times when Alice gets upset about something, and she starts to talk to Bob with pressure in her voice, her emotion showing through. Instantly, Bob's mind takes him away. He may give lip service to something she says but his safety pattern won't allow him to be present to her feelings. Alice is hurt, because she has made herself vulnerable, and tries again, but it gets worse. And finally, she speaks angrily to him — "You're not listening and you don't care!" And Bob, who has been a helpless participant in a drama he can only dimly comprehend, reexperiences the turmoil of his origins.

Had Bob read Alice's behavior as an appeal for solace, there would have been a different outcome. But how could he have when his conviction was that emotion leads to chaos? Here we see a safety pattern blocking a man from responding appropriately to another's emotions and in that way bringing on the very result he was trying to avoid.

Sally's job as a child had been to carry the whole burden of the relationship with her parents in order to ensure a continuous connection. So we can imagine she was devoting herself "well beyond reason" to her teacher precisely because she sensed, as she had with them, that her need for him was stronger than his for her. Her inflexible devotion served to shield her from perceiving the obvious disparity between their life situations until the gap between his requirements and hers became too great and the relationship, as she had known it, fell apart.

So, for all the talent she brought, for all her sophistication, and for all her expertise in pleasing others and holding on to a relationship, the event she was braced against came to pass. Her suffering was not so much over the loss of her teacher, although that was there, too, but the worst shock came from the realization that the instructions embedded in her psyche to keep her safe had, for the first time, failed her. He was going on to teach other students, but she wasn't going to be one of them. It never occurred to her that it wasn't personal.

WHEN SAFETY STRATEGIES FAIL

I cannot overemphasize the trauma of such an occurrence. Sally's neglected child had devised every possible means to avoid being rejected, because when your connection to life depends on a postcard you have little margin for error. As a child she had gone into overdrive, achieving, relating, helping people, creating. She'd left no stone unturned. She lived in the unconscious assumption that whatever came to her would come only through her own efforts. So when all those efforts and talents failed to secure a relationship, she was not just sad, she felt she was in mortal danger.

But what an opportunity her teacher's retirement provided! How else would she ever become witness to her pattern of excessive output and repeated disappointment? What would prompt her to create a wiser, more adult viewpoint where she was not the center of all meaning, negative or positive? How would she ever come to see that rejection need never be seen as personal? And without this experience, how would she let herself stop shining for long enough to realize that, without trying, she was good enough for anyone or anything her adult self might come to desire?

It didn't take long before Sally's friends, myself for one, dropped a comment or two to Sally that it was a bit of selfishness on her part to feel so undone by an old man wanting to retire. For a brief moment she viewed herself in that harsh light and was mortified. Sally was utterly allergic to being thought of as selfish. Then, as you might imagine, the "star" in her took on her own transformation with a vengeance. She steeped herself in self-help books and participated in two or more "transformational" programs where her compensatory strategies were revealed to her in an atmosphere of compassion. The energy and determination that had helped Sally survive were such that having started on a new path, she was able to find the means, within and without, to blow away the roadblocks that had arrested her growth.

The last time I spoke with her I asked her, with tongue in cheek, if she had been rejected lately. She hesitated, and then laughed at the bind the question put her in. Yes and no, she said. Yes, a number of people had said no to her on one ground or another, and no, she hadn't made those refusals mean anything negative about her.

OTHER TYPES OF SAFETY PATTERNS

Let's look at a few more examples of patterns playing out before we move on to learning in depth how to rewrite the story that generates them. The narratives that follow and the changes that occurred were the result of relatively brief encounters between the subjects and me. This was extremely heartening to me because it meant that a conversation alone might be sufficient to cause a transformation, and not a conversation that was defined as "therapy" at that. The first is the story of a woman whose family had prevented her, in her late teens, from leaving home to follow her dream on the basis that it wasn't safe for a young woman to be on her own. If we extend the notion of trauma to include experiences of being stopped in one's tracks in ways that generate fear-based stories, Sofia's would fit those criteria.

I met Sofia while I was doing training for a corporation in Monterrey, Mexico. She was the only woman on the leadership team of the company and one of the most high-flying, influential women in the country. Over a last gorgeous dinner at her home that was satisfying to every sense, she told me she was in a tug-of-war with her eighteen-year-old daughter, Theresa, over Theresa's desire to go to the United States to study. Sofia presented a cogent argument as to why she didn't trust her to be able to manage at a university so far from home, and characterized their conflict as typical of difficulties with a teenager.

Later in the evening, Theresa arrived home and I was surprised—and then mesmerized—by her grace, sophistication, and maturity. I noted to myself that she had already stepped into the competent shoes of her mother. And yes, I also saw the sparks of resentment flying between mother and daughter.

Later I questioned Sofia about the origins of her distrust of Theresa, and she eagerly shared them with me. She said it was because *her* own mother, Theresa's grandmother, had been afraid to let Sofia herself study abroad, and no matter how urgently Sofia had pleaded with her, her mother had flatly refused to let her go. "Was that the right decision for you?" I asked, but I couldn't get a thoughtful answer. I could see in her face that Theresa's request to study in the States had triggered in Sofia the memory of her mother's fear—a fear that had occurred twenty-three years earlier in a completely different era, with different customs and opportunities. Led by emotion in contradiction to her values and all reason, Sofia reflexively repeated the pattern, denying Theresa the right to attend the prestigious university that had admitted her. She registered the oddity of her decision, but immediately produced rationales to justify it: the world had become a more dangerous place; her daughter was still so immature in a number of ways; and the culture and values in the United States were antithetical to those she and her husband had been teaching Theresa.

Sofia's triggered memories had set a Dance of Parts in motion. With no adult part of Sofia available for a real conversation about the young girl's readiness to leave home, a rebellious side of Theresa rose up armed for battle in opposition to her mother's distrust, while her body implicitly absorbed her mother's anxiety in a fractal repetition* of her mother's experience. Two teenagers squared off, with no choice on either side but to fight or capitulate—that is, until Sofia became conscious of the pattern. Before I left to go back home, we had an opportunity to discuss how present situations can trigger emotions that are memories of an earlier time, but may not be pertinent to what is going on now. When I arrived home I received a gracious thank-you note from Sofia, telling me how proud

---

* Fractals are intricate patterns that repeat themselves infinitely at different scales. Fractals can be found in coastlines, clouds, snowflakes, and blood vessels, as well as many works of art. (Jackson Pollock's paintings have been analyzed and discovered to have fractal dimensions.)

she was that her smart, beautiful daughter was going to be attending university in the United States.

Patterns sourced in trauma have fear and resistance built into them, and resistance, as we are beginning to see, brings about a repetition of what you fear. The pattern, like an electric fence, may be forcing you to give such a wide berth to unwanted feelings that they appear not to exist. All you may notice is that situations in your life seem to repeat; either you decide that that's just the way life is, or you may come to the conclusion that there is something wrong with you (I pick the wrong people), or something wrong with others (nobody ever listens), or something wrong with the world at large (it's going to hell in a handbasket). Those "repetitions" that you see as clear as day are the result of a sequence: an emotional memory initiates avoidance in you, and your behavior draws a range of predictable responses from the environment. Those responses show up to you as "it's happening again." Think of how the events of Sally's life bore out the story of her safety pattern that told her she had to carry the whole burden of a relationship, and still it wasn't enough.

I discovered that these kinds of realizations need not be limited to one-on-one discussions with me or a therapist. In chapter 8 you will find out how to uncover the story that is the basis of any behavior of yours that is giving you trouble. You will be able to do this on your own, or you can enrich the process by entering a group program that is interested in tracing patterns, as Sally did.

I was running a corporate workshop to demonstrate to myself as well as others that it was possible to do this work among people who had no expectation that we would be delving into personal matters. I had spent most of the prior two hours teaching the practices of The Art of Possibility, so people understood that when things go wrong, the model of possibility instructs us to change the story that is the source of the problem, rather than do battle with the circumstances. I suggested we see if we could demonstrate this in the next twenty minutes, and asked if there happened to be a soul among the two dozen in the room brave enough to describe some aspect of life that was not working for him or her.

No one leaped up to be a guinea pig for my plan, but I could see several likely prospects as I scanned the faces around me. One or two people had gone still and thoughtful. I was willing to wait. Then a man named Sam, who worked in the finance department, volunteered. He understood that his participation would be a contribution to the group, and he said he was willing to share something that kept going wrong; but, he said, he was unable to figure out why.

Sam described how he had recently been turned down for the third time for a promotion because the corporate consensus was that he was unable to take risks appropriate to the position he sought in the company. Although he recognized some truth in the characterization, he inevitably came to the conclusion that the stance he had taken at each decision point was the wise one. He didn't agree that he was unable to act appropriately. He was at a loss as to why he kept receiving this feedback.

So we began. "What was the first bad decision you made that you can remember?" I asked. I was looking for something relevant to being risk averse. Sam named some instances in high school related to homework and one about quitting a team.

"Before that," I urged, and he came up with a couple of mild examples in his early teens. I was fairly certain the genesis of this pattern extended back before adolescence, for two reasons: one, because as he talked he wasn't exhibiting resentment or resistance, just a slight embarrassment appropriate to a younger child; and two, because none of these memories he had called up so far had any vitality in them.

Then Sam himself was quite suddenly full of life, speaking evocatively, and by this I knew he had found the origin of the story he had lived within all these years. He was three years old, he told us, and picking flowers out of the garden in the front yard of his house in Washington, D.C. They were to be a gift for his mother. He remembered how grown-up he felt when he had the idea of giving his mother a present. Pleasure radiated from his face as he

told us the story, but then quickly drained away. We soon understood why: as he stood full of joy, there in the yard with the flowers
in his hand, his father arrived home, angry. How could Sam have
picked those flowers without permission? How could he have been
so stupid, such a bad boy? Sam's body and mind seemed to freeze
as he described this scene. He was the legendary "deer in the headlights," confused, and unable to go on. Although Sam couldn't see
it yet, we in the group sensed we were in the presence of a young
child absorbing and embodying a trauma in the form of a belief. As
though in subtitles, we read, "I can't make good decisions, I'm too
stupid to trust myself," and we inferred that at that moment in
Sam's past an electric fence went up, preventing him from growing
and developing curiosity, precluding him from experimenting and
taking appropriate risks.

One problem for Sam, caught red-handed on the garden path,
was that the story we saw in subtitles had been initiated far away
from his conscious mind. So as time went on, he was unable to
challenge himself or his assumptions in any meaningful way. He
had only the tools to approach the fence and occasionally test his
strength against it by mildly asserting himself or suggesting an out-
of-the-usual course of action. But he never made a dent in the
fence. As a consequence, whenever a question arose that contained
some risk, such as whether the company should make an acquisi-
tion, or whether it should diversify its portfolio, Sam would hang
back and order more research, just to be safe. His supervisors noticed this, and though generally satisfied with Sam's work, could
not bring themselves to recommend him for a promotion.

Sam did not realize that the unseen but palpable enclosure that
limited him in so many ways had no more reality than a moat
around a castle in a fairy tale, so he never thought to question the
limitations within which he lived.

It's a problem for all of us: we are not trained to think of ourselves as governed by stories made up by younger iterations of ourselves, frozen in time. Most of us are only remotely aware that we
may be living out patterns that extend back beyond us to our ances-

tors. But even if we had an inkling, how would we set about to change them? The answer, of course, is to uncover the story and tell a new one. We will return to Sam and learn more about how to do that in chapter 8, but first, to illuminate further how stories operate and interact, and to cover all the bases, let's look at what happens when two people with all their disparate parts join up in the name of love.

CHAPTER SEVEN

The Tangle of Love

There is no journey of sincerity that a human being can take in life without the heart being broken . . . no path with real courage that doesn't lead to heartbreak—and how much energy and time we take to turn away from that [pain].

Whatever the new love, it always breaks the heart of the old belonging.

DAVID WHYTE, POET AND PHILOSOPHER

F OR MOST OF US, the absorbing and delicious experience of "falling in love" mirrors the flavor and pattern of our earliest relationship. If the tie to our primary caretaker was secure, we have a straight path to revisiting and expanding on what we came to know as intimacy. Although there will still be stories to upgrade along the way, when we fall in love, the love is likely to have resilience.

47

If our early environment, however, resulted in insecure attachment of one kind or another as Sally's and many of ours did, we will be drawn to people who display the all-too-familiar attachment style of our parents; people in whom, for better or worse, we find a sense of "home." Then in an effort to dispel the remembered danger they evoke, we follow the dictates of our childhood story: to please, perhaps, or perhaps to punish, to take over or become helpless—whatever our safety patterns dictate. So our instructions tend to bring us into waters that are similarly troubled or similarly buoyant as those of our past, and we tend to navigate them the same way.

To generalize, that compelling feeling of "being in love" with all its hopes and yearnings, however new, unique, and fascinating, is likely to bring us only the degree of security we originally experienced. If the result is satisfactory, people will enjoy life and grow. If it is too troubled they, like Alan, may stumble into a painful awareness. Then they will have the choice to transform those safety patterns that got them through childhood in the best way possible, but that compromise their lives as adults. Let's follow the course of two people searching for true partnership and lasting love who were led astray by early childhood patterns that stemmed from a sense of scarcity rather than confidence that good things would come their way.

Thomas and Mary

Thomas's father was a professional pianist whose art was the most compelling thing in his life. Although he loved Thomas, his attention to his son was intermittent at best. As a very little child, Thomas sat quietly by his father while he played the piano. After his parents divorced he stayed close to his beloved father in spirit by reflecting his interests, including the value he placed on artistic autonomy and freedom. In other words, he maintained the illusion of a secure relationship to his father by fashioning himself after him. This pattern is not now something over which he has any choice, nor would he want to. It has made Thomas brave in following his passions and free to alter a decision or change his mind.

When his parents separated and then divorced, two conditions changed in his life and greatly affected Thomas: one was his father's physical absence that now accompanied his mental detachment, and the second was the disruption in his close relationship to his mother that occurred when his mother started dating.

Now grown up, Thomas becomes involved with a young woman, Mary, who is steady and attentive, and feels safe to Thomas—the antidote to his father's self-absorption and his mother's inconstancy. Mary finds Thomas's free-spirited nature a salve for her prior experience with rule-bound, anxious, and controlling parents.

There is a wounded child in Thomas and a wounded child in Mary, as there is to some degree in most of us, each resonating with the other's similar need for attention and control. Thomas yearns for a woman to focus intently and lovingly on him and he yearns for stability. Mary's greatest hope is for unrestricted enthusiastic acceptance from a man, a man who would love her without controlling her. They have each developed a posture, an adaptation, which in the past promised to elicit the most their parents had to offer. Thomas is carefree and expressive as he was with his preoccupied father, and Mary is "good" but resistant to control of any kind, maintaining exactly the distance to be able to receive what she needed from her parents. Their adaptations foreshadow difficulty for two reasons: the patterns that were perfectly designed to bring them the attention and control they strove for in the past may not be the right tools to build a relationship in the present. But it's worse than that: those patterns that are now unconscious bring into the marriage the permanent specter of the needs they legitimately had as children—"I need more attention," "I need more control"— and drive their owners to keep seeking what they perhaps already have in a different form, or what is no longer relevant.

As time goes by, the "good girl" in Mary begins to irritate

Thomas, as does her stubborn resistance to being told what to do. What he once saw as her stability now shows up to him as rigidity, and indeed it is. Safety patterns are not adaptive; they are as resolute and single-minded as the child who first fashioned them. At the same time, Thomas's "creative" temperament that can throw all caution to the wind begins to feel random and unsafe to Mary. Her attempts to signal her distress feel entrapping to Thomas and he disregards them. For all his capriciousness, his pattern is equally as inflexible as hers. She feels that what she wants doesn't count, just as if she were a child at home with her parents, and so does he. They both become deeply disappointed when they perceive that what they were attracted to wasn't personal at all, and really had little to do with love and intimacy. It's very likely that Thomas's panache and Mary's steady distance setting both carry a similar concealed message: "Don't interfere with me because this is what keeps me safe."

It often happens when people are operating out of child parts that they experience, over time, a bewildering reversal of the magnetic field between them and become repelled by that which once attracted them. In that case, their child parts kick up such a fuss that their entire marriage seems untenable. They go into trauma mode, fleeing, or fighting, or staring like wild animals in the headlights of their decisions. In the midst of the emotional melee, it is unlikely that they can recognize that the part of each of them that feels so passionate and so threatened by the other is only a small element of who they are, and merely the memory of a long-past feeling state at that. It seems for all the world that the marriage was a colossal mistake from which there is no conceivable reprieve.

Mary's bid for control had its roots in the environment of anxiety and restraint in which she was raised, where she experienced powerlessness on a day-by-day basis. As a consequence, when she got together with Thomas, Mary was particularly keen to make some firm decisions about their future to counteract her chronic worry that life could spin out of her control. One of the plans they agreed on was that they would put off having children and both go on working after they married to build financial security. But within a year of their wedding, Thomas became deeply disillusioned with the corporate world where he was a rising creative director and fell into such a depression that the firm he was working for reluctantly accepted his resignation. It wasn't long before a couple of start-ups in the nonprofit sector came to him with offers. One of them, an Internet company, struck Thomas as perfect for him. The company's mission was to discover accomplished musicians in all corners of the world who had much to offer but no channel through which to offer it. The job would pay very little until the company could make a go of it, but it suited Thomas's interests. Thomas would be discovering musicians and showcasing them on the company Web site, as well as finding advertisers to fund the business. He knew instinctively that doing this kind of work would reenergize him and bring purpose to his life.

Mary felt blindsided. How could Thomas put emotional pressure on her to overturn their plans? The situation triggered in Mary memories of powerlessness and defeat. Her parents had been intensely involved in her life and opinionated about everything in it. Mary's room was her sanctuary, her special domain where she could arrange things to her liking, although as with most things in life, her control did not always remain absolute. It was vulnerable to a friend's curiosity, or a sibling's impulse to borrow, or her mother's fixation on keeping things clean. Her seven-year-old solution to the danger she felt at being overdirected had been to be scrupulous about planning ahead and getting people to promise a certain future. That way she would be prepared for what might be coming next. It became a survival pattern. However, seven-year-olds don't add contingencies to their solutions, and certainly Mary had no flexibility in hers. Once triggered into a defensive posture, she found it difficult to even hear what Thomas had to say.

Thomas argued cogently for the benefits of work that is inspiring and a contribution to mankind rather than work that supported a materialistic lifestyle. He assured Mary that the little start-up would thrive in time and that he would be a much happier man and a better husband to her. Eventually Mary agreed, because her rational adult mind actually was in favor of all he had to say. But the seven-year-old within her wasn't interested in compromise and would give her no rest. "He makes all the decisions," it cried. And because it was hard for the adult in Mary to justify this position, she let the child in her build the case. "Look around," the seven-year-old called out. "See, he decides where you go on vacation, he invites his friends over more often than yours. Remember how he went out and bought that expensive chair without consulting you?" Mary's resentment increased when Thomas's first paychecks reflected the business's early lack of traction. She lapsed into the pattern her mother had enacted on her as a child, punishing Thomas by going silent for days.

Responding in his father's pattern, Thomas focused single-mindedly on the new venture and avoided interactions with Mary, rendering her nightmare complete. In her mind she was back in her childhood, blocked from influencing the course of things and deprived of a voice.

So what do they do? Do they decide they are simply too different as people ever to make their marriage work, and cut their losses; or do they simply soldier on?

Perhaps they could agree to something entirely without precedent in our world: that they would put their efforts into identifying and dealing with childhood patterns until they could conduct the marriage conversation or the divorce conversation as two fully integrated adults. Imagine if they agreed not to make any decisions about their marriage until they had reached that place of internal balance, a place that is guaranteed to be loving. After all, why would you leave your entire future up to two disgruntled children?

Whether or not he understood that resistance brings about a repetition of what one is trying to avoid, imagine if Thomas were to say, "Mary, I see now that my insistence on following my dream without making sure I had your support has led *us* to the brink of divorce. I know that if I had let you in on the decision we would have found a way for me to work in a job that suits me without damaging our relationship. I really apologize." And what if Mary could say, "Thomas, I'm much less gifted at introspection than you, but I know that I tend to be too rigid. The fact is my childhood was absurdly regulated, and I seem to be trying to do the same to you. If I had resisted you less we might have come up with a better solution for both of us; but let's see how this plays out."

This is a conversation between two adults overseeing and being responsible for their child parts. What a difference it makes. What a difference it would make if we all were able to speak from such a place of consciousness.

Practices for Couples

- Make upgrading child stories part of your commitment to your partner.

- Put your attention on identifying when a child part is rising in you. You will feel yourself getting heated or agitated or overfocused on making your point. Practice dropping whatever it is that you are becoming intense about. Let it go. If you can't, say to yourself, "I am being dominated by the needs of a child in me, and it may take me awhile to calm down." Do not try to justify it by claiming that the intensity of your feeling must mean it is important.

- Never argue with the child part of your partner. Even if you "win" you will have lost ground. In addition, to do so is to bring out the child in *you*. Arguments between children, as we know, usually end with someone getting hurt.

- Try to understand what the child in your partner is saying. This is difficult because it is often a claim you consider to be a complete misrepresentation of the facts and a total misunderstanding of you. Nevertheless, let it have its say and respond with a statement such as "If I really had meant to do that to hurt you, it would be horrible. I hope you know I love you." When the child in your partner is mollified you can go on to have an adult, productive conversation. Remember, the circuitry is most malleable in the presence of love.

- Communicate through requests devoid of assumptions. For instance, ask, "Will you use this cutting board rather than the counter when you are chopping stuff?" versus "Look at the marks you made in the counter by using it as a chopping board." Or "Will you let me know when you are getting annoyed about something?" versus "How am I supposed to know when things are bothering you?" "Will you surprise me with an outing?" versus "I wish you'd take some initiative to make plans." There is almost nothing that cannot be handled well by a request and there is almost nothing you can say that won't ruin your day if you load your statement with assumptions.

- Trust that if you say something in a constructive spirit and then let it go, the relationship will seek to realign no matter what response you get in the moment, because that is the way of nature.

- Apologize for the wrongdoings of your child parts. In fact, apologize whenever you feel a rift between the two of you no matter what the cause, for the fact that you hadn't done anything up to that point to heal it. An apology does not have to imply an admission of guilt on a matter in dispute. It can be used more powerfully as a tool to affirm the primacy of our connection with others.

CHAPTER EIGHT

Rewriting the Story

H AVING EMERGED FROM BASIC training in safety patterns and their interactions, we can now begin to sort out the question of how to reset these patterns by rewriting our own narratives. Our first task is to distinguish stories that result from the way a child's mind works—which I will call, appropriately, "child stories"— from stories that were initiated by a developed mind. The latter I will refer to as "adult stories." It takes quite some skill to be able to recognize which parts of your worldview are the brilliant but rigid inventions of the three- or four-year-old within you, and which parts have the characteristic flexibility and multiple viewpoints of a story born from your accumulated wisdom.

When we have the child mind neatly distinguished from the adult mind, we can decide which stories we want to upgrade and which we can benignly leave as is. Finally, at the end of the chapter we will see an example of a child story upgrading to adult in real time (almost).

To begin, I ask you to take your critical mind off-line for a moment and accept the following claim:

When you find yourself ready to bolt from a relationship, or hanging on to one that is going nowhere, or frightened about the future, or feeling insecure in a group; when you are driving people crazy with your efforts to get things under control, or are unable to take steps that would obviously be beneficial, or are avoiding criticism of any kind, think this: *you are living in a story made up by a child.* I ask you to imagine that stories made up by the children in us, or handed down to us by the children in others, have quite different qualities and are based on fundamentally different assumptions from stories created by our integrated adult selves.

Child stories, like early theories of the universe, feature the juvenile author at the center of the drama—and dramatic these stories are. Whether describing the good or the bad, it's that "forever and ever" quality of child stories that gives them that extra theatrical flair. Sam the flower picker had it that *he* was bad, and couldn't ever (no, never) be trusted to make good decisions. Do you see how much more drama is involved in such a story than, for instance, that Sam got scolded because his father was having a bad day, and momentarily took it out on his little son? Because a child's secure base is usually only a handful of adults, his stories often have the air of crisis about them. Laced throughout are strategies to acquire approval or safety or attention from others, or to gain control. Often those child survival stories, when elaborated, carry tangible descriptions of identity: for example, "I'm a strong girl," or "I'm no leader," or "I'm the good one." Or like Sam, "I'm bad and can't be trusted to make good decisions." These conclusions are as concrete as the developmental level of the mind of the child star who created them, and to that mind they appear to represent a truth that is both absolute and timeless.

Now let's look at little Alan's strategy. "Love in Secret" was not a survival story that reflected on his character, like the story of Sam. No, it was a proactive solution to the danger of loss and rejection at a time when his universe was limited to two indispensable caretakers working at cross-purposes. Bringing his parents together on an equal footing and discussing the matter was clearly not an option for him in his toddler world, so secrecy embedded itself in his neurons. As he grew older, he brought this strategy, unchanged, to life's proliferating challenges. His conscious mind helped him to develop complex ways of hiding, but was useless in upgrading the story that thrived intact below his consciousness. In some sense he became progressively divorced from reality. For instance, as his identity formed around the strategy, he prided himself on "being a master of intimacy," a characterization he patently violated at almost every turn.

So how can you tell for yourself whether you are living in an adult narrative or in a story crafted by the mind of a child? Here is a checklist to help you to distinguish what parts of you are living in a story of growth, and where a child story is rigidly keeping things under its control:

- You are being captured by the child in you if you are certain that your views are true, and you make no attempt to question them. Whether your "information" comes from family beliefs, newspapers, or a religious manual, your certainty blocks you from learning, and changing, and being present to the flow of the world in front of you, hallmarks of the adult mind. Your certainty keeps you from moving ably with a spouse's request, perhaps, or a business adaptation, or global warming or reports of the Arab Spring. It renders you foolish enough to think you can know and bank on how our world will be in thirty years, or even that "the truth" can be found at all. Believing that you can come to certainty hinders you from having an effective relationship with evolving systems—such as the world we live in.

- Unless you have had a recent trauma, you are situated in the memories of a child when you are frequently anxious that things will go wrong, or are living your life cautiously. Fear and anxiety are the underlying emotions in the child's view of the world because for a child it is all about survival. When a danger is real and imminent, our bodies are designed to react competently; but anxiety is a sign, as well as a memory of helplessness, a pattern begun and perpetuated through our prolonged years of dependence as children, or handed down by our parents or our ancestors.

- You are living in a child part if you are regularly concerned with what others think of you. That's the dramatic I-centeredness of the child who imagines that others can see every blemish or, conversely, every aspect of perfection in her face and psyche, and further supposes that by her actions she could control what they think.

- You are in the child mind when you assume that things will repeat; that whatever was traumatic for you in the past will happen again. Such an assumption makes you approach the future with resistance, be overly cautious, and close down to life.

- You are expressing a child part when you are convinced that you have absolute needs—for a pension, for instance, or a lover, or certain comforts—and you are further convinced that your needs and desires will never change.

The assumptions and conclusions in the stories that govern the child parts of us are dramatic, I-centered, hierarchical, concrete, fear-based, scarcity-minded, identity-bound, absolute, personal through and through, and indisputable ("too late," "she won't want to," "too few resources," et cetera). However, were our minds to mature, as parts of yours and mine inevitably have, unimpeded by the implicit habits of our forefathers and by the traumas of our childhoods, they might stand on a completely different set of assumptions and convictions.

Now let's see what it looks like when we are operating from the adult narrative.

- The adult mind in us is centered in the appreciation that we have made it through childhood alive; it rests on the simple perception that we have survived and we know it to be so. Staying alive is no longer a present issue in our psyches, even while we may have to act at times with urgency on the ground.

- In the absence of survival anxiety, the mature mind is curious, devoting attention to what is not known in lieu of what is certain.

- The adult mind is open and flexible: willing to entertain new thoughts and feelings without the need to protect itself.

- The adult mind is creative: on the lookout for opportunity, and able to invent stories and move into contexts that will further our alignment with one another.

- Unthreatened by the emergence of child stories in others, the adult mind is loving and compassionate. The emotional substratum of maturity in this definition is love, joy, appreciation, gratitude, and wonder. Nothing appears as personal; whatever is happening is simply "human," and the differences between us are recognized to be far from fundamental.

- The adult mind appreciates that nothing repeats unchanged; there are no duplicate events. We will not be quite the same tomorrow as we are today. The equation "identical" happens only in our minds. Although patterns, like the seasons, repeat in form, nothing within that pattern ever happens "again." Every leaf, every snowflake, every thought is unique.

THE ADULT MIND AT WORK

When you create an adult story you are using the same data you were before, the same dots of light that made up the design of your child story, but you are arranging them differently. As you will see, those new arrangements introduce fresh information that allows you to tell a story of greater depth and maturity. Unfettered by dogma, the adult mind is free to highlight harmony and connection over discord and disconnection, and by doing so cause a shift toward integration on scales that range from dinner table conversations to battles erupting around the world.

The mature mind, in this model, attempts to observe life from the viewpoint of all sentient beings, whether from their shoes or hooves or wings. From this adult practice, fair-mindedness and collaboration arise naturally. Hierarchy is seen to be a phenomenon of nature but not an imperative. In this stance we are all leaders: we assert that we have the capacity to enroll others and move things, however gradually, in the direction that is best for all.

The "adult" is aware that appearances are not fixed, but subject to the story she is telling. When things go wrong for her, the place she turns to look is not out there, but inside herself, to the assumptions that are governing the way reality appears to her. She accepts that the source of change and transformation is in her narrative, not in the world at large.

She experiences that the rewriting of the interior narrative instantly conjures up an altered external world aligned with the new story. In other words, she understands that if she changes her story, she is guaranteed to experience life differently and be drawn to act accordingly.

The adult mind seeks to bring itself into alignment with the movement of our universe, opening to new information, letting go of resistance, looking for what it hasn't seen before, searching and listening for evolving order. And for the adult, love inevitably appears as the context of it all.

Rewriting the Child's Story

When Sam, who remembered so well his joy at plucking flowers for his mother and then the terrible consequences, was able to see how closely his interpretation followed the elements of a child story, he could consider various alternative stories from an expanded adult frame of mind. Others in the group joined in with suggestions for a more mature narrative. Maybe his father had simply had a hard day? Perhaps his father had spent time and effort on cultivating the garden and reacted too harshly for that reason? Maybe his parents had been in an argument, and Sam had taken the brunt?

As soon as Sam heard the last suggestion, forgotten incidents of parental conflict came instantly to his mind. Of course! He had felt the tension in the household over the years. He remembered his father accusing his mother of using Sam to keep him at bay. Indeed, this new interpretation had much more of the ring of truth to him than the old, and obviously childish, one. Sam began to laugh freely as his synapses made new connections and his neurons laid new tracks. Now he saw himself as a sweet kid trying to make sense and safety out of a conflict his parents had enacted for years. It had nothing to do with him!

Was Sam's latest story correct, that his father had seen his little son clutching the flowers and become irritated at the closeness between mother and son? We have no way of knowing, but accuracy is far from the point here. What is important is that the new story had jumped a category, and that it had an authentic ring for Sam. It was composed of elements from an adult's rather than a child's mind, so no matter what interpretation he had landed on, it would serve him by allowing him to let go of the idea that he was personally responsible for his father's anger. Such stories are works in progress, and remain ever open to revision.

The group saw the transformation in Sam. He was able to appreciate and speak about the big heart of his three-year-old self, almost as though he were his own father. He was already creating synaptic sequences and pathways that would take him over and beyond the boundary of the old electric fence. As people took the cue from Sam and began to think about their own stories, we saw in Sam the courage he had been missing. He was, after all, providing leadership for the people in the room, and he had definitely stepped out of the survival mode, into strength and freedom.

So far, Sam's decision making had been fixated on keeping himself safe. The very fact that he could say with a laugh that his father's anger "had nothing to do me" in his new story is an indication that his perspective had broadened and he was no longer situated at the center of a child's universe looking out. What could be a better indication that he was ready to achieve a wiser and more dynamic balance between caution and risk?

> *Everyone thinks of changing the world, but no one thinks of changing himself.*
>
> LEO TOLSTOY

Some do, Mr. Tolstoy.

CHAPTER NINE

Upgrading Stories from Child to Adult

Aт тне risk of repeating a story that some readers may have heard before, I include this iconic tale because its message is so very apt for our journey.

It was Wednesday and lunchtime at a construction site. Two workers, Bob and Jim, sat down together and opened their lunch boxes. Jim noticed that Bob became agitated as he unwrapped his sandwich. "Tuna fish salad?" Bob exclaimed. "I don't *like* tuna fish salad," and he indignantly dropped the sandwich into the Dumpster. Jim offered him part of his own lunch and they finished the half hour in conversation. Thursday at the noon meal, the two men again sat together and as soon as they opened their lunch boxes, Bob startled Jim by beginning to shout. "Peanut butter? What am I, a kid? I hate peanut butter!" and he flung his sandwich unceremoniously in the trash. On Friday Jim made sure to find Bob at the break, curious to see how this day's meal would go. Bob unwrapped his sandwich; again the agitation, again the shouting: "Ham and cheese? I despise ham and cheese!" and once more Bob hurled his lunch into the garbage.

Jim finally screwed up his courage and intervened. "Bob," he said, "I don't mean to intrude, but why don't you have a word with your wife if you don't like what she puts in your lunch box?"

"You leave my wife out of this," said Bob. "I make my own sandwiches."

How hard is it to see that we live in a life of our own making? If you witnessed the evidence as clearly as Jim did, would you still complain? At this stage in our evolution, we just aren't designed to appreciate that everything that each of us sees and experiences is the product, one way or another, of our own invention and assumptions. How many times will we stumble before we start to become aware? Quite a bit, I'm afraid, if my experience is any indication.

When I was working on *The Art of Possibility* I used to go on weekends in fall and winter to a cabin south of Boston to do the writing. The cabin is on a pond, in front of a cranberry bog, and surrounded by acres of conservation land. It provided everything I needed to get my work done: freedom from interruptions, a relaxed atmosphere, beauty, and quiet. As I looked forward to my very first weekend in my recently purchased hideaway I was extremely excited. I was going to spend three days in an environment in which nothing would disturb my concentration.

That first Friday morning, I packed the car with the odds and ends of my work, and all the food my dog, Luna, and I would need for the long weekend, and we started off. When we arrived at about eleven a.m., I carted the stuff into the house and responded to Luna's insistence that we go for a walk. And what a lovely walk it was—the leaves of the oak trees had turned a dark brilliant red, and the grasses along the edge of the bog were shimmering in ecstasy.

What happiness! When I returned to the cabin, I attended to housekeeping matters. I put out a bowl of water for Luna, plugged in the computer, brought out my papers, and I made myself some lunch. After lunch, when I had done a dish or two and put more things away, I felt a little sleepy, and since it had been a busy week, I felt fine about taking a nap. After my little sleep, I made coffee, and I stared out the window. I noticed that the daylight was fading. In an effort to avoid anxiety around the fact that I hadn't yet accomplished anything, I turned my attention to the computer.

It did not look inviting.

But I forced myself to sit down, and permitted myself to play a soothing game of solitaire as preparation for writing. With extreme difficulty I eked out an introductory paragraph, after which, without any intention to do so, I found myself at the refrigerator. I poured myself a glass of wine, fed the dog, made dinner, put sheets on the bed, and I figured there was just time for another walk before calling it a day.

A variation of this schedule—a little uninspired writing, a couple of walks, quite a lot of rearranging of papers and books—took hold over the next two days while, under a relatively calm exterior, I became increasingly frantic. By the time I left the cabin, I was in quasi-despair, but ready to try again the following Friday.

The second weekend, I arrived steeled to make myself sit in front of that desk. I had several plans for fixing the problem, a problem that I was hoping wouldn't turn into writer's block. The schedule was to be this: walk the dog at seven a.m., eat breakfast and put all papers in order before start time, and sit down to work for four hours with one break before lunch. I was to avoid the refrigerator except at designated times.

As we know, what you resist persists. What actually happened was that hardly had I sat down when I was veering away from the computer on one excuse or another. I frequently visited the refrigerator, and several times walked out of the house, to the dog's delight, without really intending to do so. All the power seemed to reside in my headstrong unconscious, rendering my own conscious will completely impotent. At this point it was clear to me that I had genuine writer's block, just as if it had been fashioned from granite. I called a friend and told her about it, and she tried to help. "Perhaps you are sitting too long," she said. "Take breaks every twenty minutes." In my demoralized state I left early on Sunday, beating the traffic back to Boston.

Over the third weekend, I hit a crisis point. From my desk in the cabin I shouted aloud, "This is *hopeless*," setting Luna's pointed ears twitching in alarm. And indeed it was hopeless. I was bearing down with my will to overcome a problem I had created myself out of several disempowering narratives but, unlike the construction worker, I didn't realize I was making my own sandwiches. One story was simply that I wasn't doing what I was supposed to be doing, and another that I had developed "writer's block." I was orienting to these constructions as though they were reality, not a meal of my own making. No wonder I was becoming desperate.

I took a deep breath, and gave up. Finally I remembered what my work is about. If I was ever to get down to it, I would be writing about changing the story, not changing myself or battling the world as it appeared to me through the lens of that story, so I called to Luna and left the cabin and took (another) long walk.

"What story am I acting out?" I finally asked myself, and in my mind I surveyed the elements of "writer's block" and began to question my definitions of things. "What is writing?" was one of my first questions and it held the key. I was defining writing very, very narrowly, as sitting at a computer and producing words. I continued walking and walking and relaxed my mind. And this is the new definition of writing, and the new story, that I (or it, or Divine Intervention or Nature herself) came up with: "Everything I do at the cabin—from the time I get out of the car in front of the cranberry bog until the time I get into the car to go back to Boston—is writing. Walking the dog is writing, having lunch is writing, certainly taking a nap is writing, and a night's sleep is writing. Reading the newspaper and playing solitaire are both writing, and punching the keys down on the computer is also writing."

Prior to this moment, I had had flashes of deep understanding that the world is invented, that it unfolds in the story you tell, so even though I was prone to forget this, I was at a great advantage. My understanding allowed me to "believe in" my reasonably plausible new story. But soon something rather miraculous happened to give it grounding. Memories and evidence that fit the new story, but not the old child one, came tumbling into my mind. For instance, I had heard that our whole bodies absorb about eleven million bits of information per second, but that the conscious mind can process only approximately sixteen of them. That's a ratio in the range of a million to one! Obviously our conscious minds cannot be counted on to process very much. So it seemed clear that writing a book about possibility was probably not going to be done primarily with the few bits my conscious mind would be able to work with. It was going to take the whole of me and then some; and suddenly the new story "Everything I Do at the Cabin Is Writing" made all the sense in the world. I saw that walking in the woods with all this richness of information flowing in was part of writing. And I saw that letting the unconscious do its processing in sleep was obviously part of the venture, and that the sensual feel of an animal's fur under my hand was, also, part and parcel of writing.

That, as I can testify, was the end of "writer's block" and the start of a focused, passionate, and productive period. To write a book about possibility I had only to hang out in this magical cabin surrounded by fields and woods, listening to birds at dawn, and watching swans glide by on the pond. I had only to do what my surroundings prompted me to do, and they prompted me to write chapters and go for walks, take naps, wash dishes, and dream. The book got written, and as our editor, Carol Franco, said at the end of the process, "It was accomplished not simply with hard work, but with spirit."

GUIDELINES FOR UPGRADING YOUR STORIES

When you truly fathom that you can take any pattern or story that has been holding you back and transform it into a possibility story, you have the world at your fingertips. You won't get far, however, if you hedge your bets. It is necessary to declare across the board that you live in stories—all of you, all of the time. You may want to address only those that are holding you back, of course. Here are some avenues that may lead to uncovering them:

- Think of times you have said, "Don't try to change me, that's just the way I am." Capture what you mean by "that's the way I am," and what it implies about what you can and can't do. You will see that it is a story open to revision.

- List some conditions you are convinced are critical to your happiness—for example, "I can't really relax until I know everyone is safe (or there is enough money in the bank, or people around me are happy, or I have finished my work)." Note where the story comes from, and how you have memorialized, over time, a condition you were once worried about, or were too young and powerless to change. Notice, too, how disempowered you are by your story.

- Examine, one by one, the words you are using to define a problem that confronts you. Redefine any words that are causing fear in you, or resistance, or that imply a struggle, until the struggle and fear subside. For example, while guest-conducting an orchestra that was new to him, my co-author of *The Art of Possibility*, Ben Zander, felt blocked by a woman violinist whom he saw as resisting him, who appeared to be quite cynical about the rehearsal process. Then it occurred to Ben to examine the word "cynic," and he came up with a very plausible definition that opened the door to an easy relationship. He declared a cynic to be "a passionate person who doesn't want to be disappointed again." From then on he felt entirely aligned with the passionate player in her who was reluctant to give her all to every guest conductor who might foist poor interpretations and shoddy music-making on the orchestra. By the time of the performance, all trace of the "cynic" in her had disappeared, overwhelmed by her newly released passion.

- Examine your political leanings or religious beliefs in the light of the elements in the description of adult and child stories. See whether you are certain that you know the truth (child) or whether you are open to new information (adult). Notice how hierarchical, or fear based, your convictions are, or how flexible you are in altering them. Our leaders in both fields may be playing to the child in us that craves certainty and right answers. How much better for the leaders of the church or the body politic to have adult partners.

- Look for elements in situations you avoid that have the ring of the child and lend themselves to being upgraded to "adult." For instance, if you often declare to yourself (and others) that you can't take criticism, and find yourself dodging it at all costs, you might notice that your story implies that there are people out there who want to put you down or punish you. There may, indeed, have been those in the past. You may have had a critical parent or been subject to a harsh parochial education. But to keep living within the electric fence of "I can't take criticism" leaves you a victim in a drama about malevolent authorities. An example of an upgraded narrative could be that what you are labeling as "criticism" is an intimate partner's attempt to clear the air between the two of you so that you are closer, or a friend's bumbling but well-intentioned way of supporting you.

- Widen the frame in your search for an adult story to include what others might be feeling, as well as how your story is related to your ancestry, your culture, or what is happening around the world. Keep at it until you are no longer the hero, or the victim, or even the one who you think is performing the act in question.

In a workshop I was conducting with the leadership team of a company, one of the fellows put forward that he had a problem with his secretary, whom he portrayed as impossible to manage, messy, lazy, and not willing to improve. I asked him to describe the exact actions that led to his interpretations—the kind of thing you could see on film. In the process, and with others adding whatever experience they had had with the woman, we discovered new information. It turned out that she had lost her husband a couple of years before, and then had been demoted to a position where she was reporting to a woman with whom she had previously been on an equal level. So we arrived at a picture of an employee who was scared to lose her job, and reluctant to have conversations with the woman to whom she reported, and was not acknowledged for the impossible position she was in. Others around the table began to chime in that they felt she had been improving recently, and they saw her as producing the goods when she was allowed to handle things on her own.

Her boss was astounded by how radically, with a wider frame around it, the picture changed. In the space of fifteen minutes the secretary had shifted in his view from "lazy" to "productive," from "unmanageable" to "maintaining her dignity"; from "messy" to "grieving"; and from "unwilling to develop" to "growing at a fast pace for what she had to handle." It is the mark of a competent (and adult) leader that he can embrace a new reality that clears a logjam swiftly and with grace.

On my first weekends in the cabin, remember, I was operating on the assumption that writing was putting words on a page, and you got them there by being disciplined and using willpower. People in my world were either successes or failures, and I was definitely failing. The new, transformed story with its frame enlarged to include the woods and fields, as well as the conscious and nonconscious mind, produced a collaborative world of which I was a part, but one in which I wasn't the main character. I wasn't the heroine, or the lazy one. I had no dramatic role to play. I was a person whose behavior was being sourced by a combination of context and commitment. Immediately, on settling on the story, I felt relaxed, joyous, and open—earmarks of an adult narrative.

Let's look at some of our other stories and how they transitioned from child to adult.

The child aspect of Sam the flower picker's story was that it was all about his mistake and how stupid he was. The story shifted to an adult form and produced the laughter of relief when he brought in parental strife as an explanation, independent of his actions. Alan Spingold had decided that to be safe he had to give himself over separately to irreconcilable parties without contradicting either, and without risking anything by developing his relationships further. His powerlessness dissipated when he truly recognized that he had been living in a story designed by a three-year-old to handle a toddler's anxiety. The new story, bolstered by his competence-building practices, had him living in a world he defined as reliably connected and rich with relationships, where there was the time and space for him to be himself. Sofia, the Mexican businesswoman, made an inappropriate attempt to protect her daughter from dangers that existed only in her recollection of a different era. When she became conscious that she had been trapped by nothing more than a memory, she was able to let go of her fears and let go of her daughter, too, and experience appropriate pride and joy.

Be sure your new definitions are plausible and result in the experience of instant alignment with the world around you. You can't create a story in opposition to anything you continue to hold to be true. If you are convinced your mother didn't love you, your mind won't let you get away with saying she did, but it might accept that she loved you as much as she ever loved anything, or it might allow that her own suffering kept her insulated from tender feelings of any kind.

Usually an upgrade from the child story in question is accomplished by a combination of analysis and imagination, but occasionally a story will change and become adult under special conditions of heightened feeling, as though by divine intervention. The following is such an example.

An Instantaneous Upgrade

A client of mine experienced a sudden upgrading of *her* child story in a moment of extreme emotion in the universally intensified environment that accompanies birth and death. Her new story changed the landscape of her life.

Carol stayed with her mother through the last stages of a painful illness. During this time, her mother exhibited an exaggeration of her normal behavior, alternating between sweetness and disparaging outbursts, which Carol was unfortunately quite used to.

Over the hours of their last night together there was tenderness between them, but it was also a very difficult time for both because Mrs. Hawthorne was struggling so hard for breath. Toward three a.m. Carol leaned against the foot of the bed, exhausted. "I don't think we can do this much longer," she observed to herself and was instantly aware of the momentousness of the thought. Her intuition was that she and her mother were taking this journey together and if she let go, her mother would as well.

Shortly after dawn, Mrs. Hawthorne's breathing faltered and then ceased. They had reached the dreaded fork in the road. Carol stayed present with her mother through the next epic, emotionally charged passage of only a few minutes' duration, stroking her hair and telling her that she loved her and, at a loss for anything else, reciting a comforting poem.

Then a very surprising thing happened. Into Carol's head came this sentence, a revelation: "Oh, you loved your children, but you didn't really want to be a mother." With those words, almost half a century of struggle blew away like smoke in the wind, leaving her curiously and deeply peaceful.

What happened? Remember that in traumatic, momentous, or highly emotional states, our brains are ripe for change. For nearly half a century, Carol had followed a pattern that emerged out of the disorganized attachment she experienced in her earliest infancy. Carol had constructed a child's-eye view of what it was to be a mother, a highly idealized version of parenthood. A mother, she thought, and secretly longed for, should be reliable, even-tempered, available without fail, and should at all times live up to her word. You can see how far short a woman of any emotional instability might fall from this ideal! Starting from as young as three or four, Carol had decided that her mother was desperate to be able to function as Carol desired, and she had been on a crusade to teach her to be that kind of mother. She lived with this narrative, unchanged, for fifty long years.

Carol's story, as you can see, was childcentric, based on the emotional conviction that this idealized mothering was critical for her survival, and everyone else's. So her thankless mission, doggedly pursued, was that of making her mother a "competent" parent, without realizing that she, Carol, actually needed almost nothing, beyond her childhood years, of this "mothering" she thought she required. While for the most part Carol sported a sunny disposition, at the times when she felt compelled to educate her mother, who showed no ambition to "improve," she became argumentative and aggressive and caused untold family stress.

With the advent of the words that came into her head at the highly charged moment of her mother's death, the old child story was replaced by a new adult story, and Carol took one enormous leap. The new adult story was that it was okay that her mother hadn't followed the idealized path Carol had laid out for her: "You hadn't ever really wanted to be (my kind) of mother." It was a path designed by a child, after all, an infant on a mission to heal her fear of perishing from disconnection, but completely at odds with the current realities of adult life. It hadn't occurred to her until that moment that her mother, though often bewildered by Carol's intense campaign, didn't feel particularly inadequate as a mother except when Carol was railing at her; so as far as she was concerned, she didn't need to be saved. After all, her grown children were doing awfully well by anyone's standards.

Carol saw now that a person could make such a choice—"I choose not to be a perfect parent (or friend or lover)"—and accept the consequences, and the miracle was that that applied to Carol as well. It let her off the hook of her own perfectionism so that she could relax and be just as good as she really was, and that somehow left her feeling warmly connected and remarkably secure.

The new story changed her memories, too. While she listened to other women talking about what had gone wrong in the families in which they grew up, Carol no longer had any energy to add to the dialogue. When she thought of her mother, she thought of her imagination and wit and of loving times. She was occasionally reminded of temper tantrums and flying objects, but without the old intensity. She had a spacious feeling that all was right with the world. She gave up on the idea of improving her husband and children as well, and in this modern adult fairy tale, lived happily ever after—or at least so far, and of course not without some ups and downs.

Something truly extraordinary happens when you rewrite or upgrade a narrative that has had you humming along in a certain pattern for years and years. It's as though you've suddenly grown tall enough, finally, to see out the window where the riches of adult life lie in full view. Sam was finally liberated from his shame over picking the flowers, and grew to take on a new category of risk. I was able to stop worrying about whether I would be up to the task of writing, and gained a whole new outlook on how things really work.

Upgraded stories upgrade you. When you shift a story from the child mode to an adult mode, you move along the continuum, too.

Your perspective expands, frustration gives way to empowerment, and your heart becomes more open and generous.

There are, as we have seen, all kinds of stories: stories that draw you into a life of abundance, and stories that take you tumbling into fear and scarcity. You now have some tools to notice the stories that are generating the life you are living, and methods to discover where they come from. You also have a minihandbook for adopting new ones, or rewriting those that have kept you imprisoned in childhood—stories that fail to light up your life or the lives of others. So go ahead and get started!

PART II
YOU
On Behalf

of Others

Now we are heading into an arena that features you, the reader, as an instrument for change. This is very tricky, because as you may have noticed, most of us spend an inordinate amount of time and effort trying to change other people, whether it be a spouse, one's children, the neighbors, an employee, or the entire Middle East.

Some of the techniques we use to try to change people are management, patience, the "do as I say" method, exclusion, loving manipulation, bribery, and ultimatums. Some of these approaches work well some of the time, but often they produce a backlash. In this section we are going to focus on transformation, not change. When we speak of transformation we are always speaking of systems, or fields, not about anyone's personal efforts to improve. We are looking at how one person's behavior, when altered by a shift in perspective, simultaneously affects others and initiates new feedback loops.

Remember the lazy, unmanageable, messy corporate secretary who had no desire to improve? You saw how additional information, such as the fact that she was recently widowed and had been demoted at work, served to change the story so that she appeared to her boss and colleagues as, "given all that, *productive,* and handling things well." You can imagine that, with the new story in place, people's behavior changed around her with no effort on their part.

So if you are going to cause a shift in another, you accept that you are obliged first to bring about a shift in yourself, a transformation, which is equivalent to walking into a new story; and you may keep on experiencing little shifts as interactions take place in the new narrative. The world will occur differently to you, and therefore you will act differently, and people will act differently in response. With your new perspective, they will appear to be changed anyway, even though they do nothing at all. Are you interested? Are you ready?

CHAPTER TEN

Walking Stories

I T WAS ONE OF those rare spring days in London that you more often read about than have the opportunity to enjoy, with a blue sky and charming little puffs of cloud. I was heading toward the zoo from the south end of Regent's Park, duly admiring the vast assemblies of daffodils lining the walkways. Then I looked up and noticed that the path ahead was dotted with people coming toward me. But what astonished me was that each person's appearance struck me as unusually rich in texture, remarkable, and utterly unique. Here was a man in a neat gray suit clutching a briefcase, walking slightly tilted, his mouth set. I noticed that everything about him matched. What perfection! His eyes darted toward me, then away, and he continued the angled momentum of his journey. A woman with poufed hair in a capacious green coat offset with a pinkish scarf came along next, glancing around cheerfully, her outfit and hairdo echoed in the shape of her eyeglasses. Could this be, I thought? Each person appeared as a work of art, unimaginably expressive. As though they were walking onto a fashion runway for my delight, a couple moved by me in costumes that hinted of the hunt, her eyes fixed on the horizon, his on her, their steps jaunty, their faces expectant.

At this point I was so energized and amused by each passing pedestrian that I was certainly smiling broadly if not laughing outright—not, I realized, a very British thing to be doing. I felt as though we were all in on a delightful game. People are walking stories! Every person I passed on my stroll to the zoo was a consummate mime artist, elaborating his tale with Chaplinesque genius. How had I never seen this about people before? How could I have missed it? I beamed at each passerby who had revealed himself so intimately, and each one, in precisely the way his role dictated, registered my joy by looking away, or seeming alarmed, or perhaps offering a pleasant half smile.

That stroll through Regent's Park highlighted for me that we are indeed stories in motion; we are patterned appearances. Down to the smallest gesture, our actions and expressions are perfectly coordinated with our narrative, the world as we personally perceive it. And by this phenomenon we enroll others into the "truth" of who we are, such that our identities are reinforced and given greater credence through our relationships. But that morning I saw through to something fundamental behind the dramas of people's lives, and I wasn't fooled into thinking that the listing, rigid gentleman I first encountered was unbending at his core. I saw that he was acting out the "story" of his life, and he was doing it so well that I was prompted to give him a standing ovation.

So it occurred to me that another inroad on changing patterns is to take with a grain of salt the story someone is presenting: the story that she is timid, or he is very smart, or he is incapable in some way or another—in fact a person's entire presentation, his view of reality that is evident in every gesture. I don't mean oppose it or critique it. I mean love the brilliance of it as an appearance on life's stage, and in a straightforward way call on and call forth the person behind it, who you say is all possibility.

Behind the Walking Story

You might think it would be easy to call to mind an abstraction of a person of infinite possibility underlying each story in motion, but it turns out that most of us are able to do so only selectively and sporadically. When we engage with people whose values and habits feel right and familiar, like fellow dog walkers in the park, a smile one way or another springs us into productive partnership. However, even with such people with whom we click, there is always the chance that they will express an opinion, such as, "I don't think any of us should let our dogs off-leash," or do something that falls afoul of our own story of the way things should be, and send us into resistance. And then we don't know what to do to make things right, and feel helpless or irritated, or we set a polite distance. It takes only an instant to have us forget that it was our own open, warm way of being that made collaborators out of them in the first place, and it is now the resistance in our way of being that has turned their mild differences, say, with regard to dog rearing, into emotional deal breakers.

At that point the idea of changing them is likely to come to mind. But we know we can't change people, right? No matter how helpful or stern we try to be, no matter how thoughtfully we set boundaries, no matter how smart or patient we are, they stay pretty much the same (except that they now feel blamed). Right?

Well, no. This phenomenon of perceived stasis occurs only because we forget that it is the *quality of our being* that is transformative, not our actions. Another way of saying this is that it is our story about the person that locks him into appearing a certain way. If we want to change how we experience him, we can reliably do so only by changing our story about him. This is a two-stage phenomenon. When you wrest yourself from the convincing novel of a person's presentation and relate to the essence, the possibility you say is within him, you will stand with an open heart and he will appear to be different, while still doing the same sorts of things that may have triggered you just moments before. Eventually, your consistency of being and your open receptiveness will have an effect of some kind, because they constitute a transformational environment. We don't know how people will change around you, but they will change; and so will you. We do know that they will not anymore appear as antagonistic and you will no longer be ill disposed toward them. You may even feel warm and embracing.

So if you aspire to be an agent for change, beyond giving smart advice, look to your own narratives. Remember that a person is a story in motion made up of many parts, and beyond that story is an unexpressed infinite self, waiting to be activated by the open channel of your being. Keep in mind that creating freedom around your own patterns is key to others' liberation from theirs.

GOING THE INTERNAL DISTANCE

Years ago, I was a participant in an outdoor team-building activity, known as a ropes course, that vividly revealed to me the power of upgrading one's own story as a catalyst for transformation all around. I was involved in a challenging run that took us up a mile-long hill, with special dispensation to do so as a walker because of a bad knee. Even so, I occasionally found myself nearly passing some lagging runners, but just at that moment I would slow down and stay just slightly behind. Odd! The course was intended for people to do some self-reflection, and with that permission, I was able to ask myself what might be holding me back. I knew at once that I didn't want to make a runner uncomfortable by passing her, but what I hadn't seen was how thoroughly my body was programmed to slow down if such an eventuality presented itself. When I forced myself to try to move against it I felt surprising resistance. And then I remembered one incident after another where, being the youngest child in the family, I suffered the unsettling consequences of the rare times when I came out on top. I didn't notice it on the climb, but it is obvious that I was viewing the other runners as nothing more than their stories. The slower ones were occurring for me as fixed at a certain speed and sadly unable to tolerate being overtaken by a walker. I was acting as though it were up to me to save them from moral ruin.

The insight that I was afraid of the negative results of winning over people who (I said) should have been winning over me wasn't quite enough in itself to change the pattern, until I saw that I was generating a complicated game that was all about victory and loss. Then the obvious hit me — and the context surrounding me changed. That wasn't the point of the uphill run! We were all equally privileged to participate in a structure that would allow us to see what was holding us back. It had nothing to do with who was the fastest. And with that realization, a story that had governed my life shifted, upgraded, and went from child to adult.

On the next run my body as well as my heart knew what to do, and both stepped into a completely new pattern. As I easily inched past some slower runners I called out with humor and affection, "Come on, you can do it. Don't let a walker pass you." And right there my complicated and childish competitive posture of letting others win changed into an exuberant and powerful embrace of my running mates. I simply hadn't seen that as an option before because it lay outside the borders of my previous story. It was a huge breakthrough for me and, as it turned out, for others as well, who in response transformed a victim story into one of empowerment and made a discontinuous change in the time it took them to cover the mile.

METAMORPHOSIS

When I discussed this concept with Karen T., the CEO of a business that had hired our Possibility Team as consultants, she was keen to provide me with a perfect example of seeing through a person's presentation to the possibility beyond. Something had occurred in her early days volunteering as a teacher in a small ballet school that stayed with her, informing her choices and integrating with her methods of working.

Karen and two other young women were preparing a dozen little ballet dancers, ages four to nine, for a performance for family and friends. Karen had chosen a scene from Saint-Saëns's *Carnival of the Animals*, in large part to provide an opportunity for the parents, who were eager to help, to come together with their sewing machines and construct a bevy of animal costumes.

A dilemma arose in the rehearsal process. One little girl, Julia, age six, was exceptionally awkward for her age, an element that had been easily accommodated in the classroom, but became more problematic in the theater. When the children were arrayed in four rows onstage, Julia's clumsiness was obvious even in the back row. The two other teachers were convinced that the child should sit out the performance, one even justifying her opinion by declaring it too risky to include her because she might fall off the stage. Karen was torn, but then pulled herself up short. "Our job here," she thought, "is to make all the children successful," and found herself quite unwilling to participate in the unnecessary destruction of any more of the child's self-esteem. Anyway, she thought Julia might become more aware of herself and her body in the process of acting a new role. At the same time, Karen found herself at a standoff with the others, who clearly didn't want Julia to ruin the performance they had worked so hard on. For a moment Karen felt trapped by the conflicting demands—not an unfamiliar feeling for a young woman used to serving the needs of others. However, this time the feeling of pressure showed up as a sign to her that all their egos were involved: the other teachers were worried about looking good and she was worried about being rejected if she went against them. With that thought she felt a surge of energy—they were all in this together!—and all the weightiness dropped away. "This is theater," she reminded herself. "It's all about creativity! We can make up whatever we want!" She ventured the suggestion that if they were to create an additional role for Julia, and make her, say, a butterfly, Julia couldn't go wrong—with big enough wings, she could flit and stumble and nothing would be seen to be amiss.

Karen's coworkers responded to her novel idea with good spirit, and by and by the costume team got to work making a pair of gorgeous butterfly wings for the awkward little girl.

The children rehearsed several times in their costumes in order to be able to manage their tails, trunks, and hooves, so Julia had many chances to try out her wings. To the teachers' surprise, the "indisputably clumsy child" got so good at moving her arms (and her feet) in the right steps to the music that by the time of the performance she had won a place in the second row, easily visible to the audience. What an excited, happy little girl she was. After the performance, when the clapping died down and everyone dressed to leave, Julia quietly declined to take off those beautiful wings. So her parents asked for special permission to let Julia take them home. They were a part of who she had become.

Twenty years later, Karen was still excited to tell the tale. It was an experience that shaped her life, she said, and it showed up again and again as she grew a family and then a business. She felt she had stumbled—no pun, I think, intended—on a profound truth about how the world works. The little bit of insight she had come to about her own ego had eased her concerns about being left out and allowed her to stand up boldly for what she saw was desirable and possible. Her unalloyed commitment freed her mind, allowing her to find a fail-proof solution that worked for everyone "outside the box." The greatest lesson they all learned, she was happy to say, was to look beyond appearances and connect lovingly with who a person could be, "then give it everything you've got."

It is so easy to believe your perception must be accurate when you see qualities in a person as plain as day, like negativity, shyness, or disorderliness, especially when the one you are reflecting upon is someone you love, or at least someone in whose life you are entwined. When we observe in such a person a "trait" and lock on to it, it is hard for our minds to refute it, or even to hold it in question. This is partly because we are looking through the lens of our own stories, but also because the evidence for a trait you've identified, like your child's ADD, just keeps growing and expanding under your discerning eye. Stories, you remember, are fields that showcase and also draw in evidence — but not any evidence, only that which supports them in a confirming loop.

Most efforts to change others leave people feeling criticized and made wrong. And they're right to feel that way: the very desire to change another human being signifies that underneath your concerned exterior, you *are* feeling critical. It means you have no doubt he is exactly the way you see him, and you are having trouble embracing him as you see him to be. So when you have the impulse to change another person, look to see if you are being hijacked by a walking story of your own, because clearing your own will allow you to see the path for others, just the way Karen the ballet teacher hit upon making up a new role for Julia that would free her to develop while she herself stayed connected to her doubting colleagues, or the way I found myself urging people on in the mile-long run. These actions were not planned; they were spontaneous responses of people who had momentarily come to transparency in themselves and saw through to what was possible. So if you are excited by such a prospect, use the instructions for upgrading your stories. Employ your X-ray vision and become an open field for expansion and growth.

CHAPTER ELEVEN

"AS OUR CIRCLE OF knowledge expands," Einstein is quoted as saying, "so does the circumference of darkness surrounding it." What this means is that we will never know for sure whether we have found the truth. The scientists, writers, philosophers, engineers, children, and artists among us will always be able to invent additional theories, make up new stories, and design paradigms that will reveal new realities; and those latest "truths" may well contradict those that once had us so convinced. It also means a death knell for the parts of each of us that are opinionated, advice giving, and full of certainty. A blessing, if you ask me.

Just the same, how often do you find yourself being pretty certain about what you think people should do to forward their lives, but just not sure how to go about getting them to do it? Let's face it; we human beings are absolutely riveted by the opportunity to diagnose a situation out there and get it right. I once listened to three Nobel Prize–winning economists discussing the downturn in 2008. Each of them had a strong, airtight, and divergent explanation of why it had happened, and when pressed by the moderator, all admitted they hadn't had a clue that it was coming down the road. Huh? But in forming our tightly held opinions, e.g., "that company will never succeed" or "Lisa is a fool if she leaves Tim," how reliably do we look to our own stories to see how and why we formed such beliefs?

The next story, about an old friend of mine named Bruce, illustrates how he lost his way with his wife because of his laudable desire to help her. In his eagerness, however, he confused what he saw on the surface, the overt narrative, with the possibility behind it. When we make the mistake of assuming that what we see is true, our attempts to "help" almost always amount to efforts to fix and change the other's unconscious constructed reality, which I have been referring to as a "walking story." Such efforts inevitably promote stubborn resistance in the one to be fixed, and render the "helper" the very picture of helplessness.

Bruce and I had been out of touch for several years when he called me just prior to one of our college reunions. As we were catching up on the usual subjects — careers, marriage, and children — he shared with me very proudly that his wife, Alice, was a fabulous cabinetmaker who was recently getting requests for her work from all over their state. But as we talked on, he admitted a problem. "She's never satisfied with her work — and she keeps thinking she's not good enough, no matter how many people tell her otherwise." I could hear Bruce sigh. "Her lack of self-confidence is beginning to have a negative effect on our income and even our personal life because she's afraid to ask for a proper fee. I want to make her realize she's a skilled and talented artist, whose work is worth much more than she thinks." As much as Bruce tried to appear loving and concerned, his frustration showed through.

As Bruce conveyed his picture of Alice, did you, the reader, get the sense that he had her tightly wrapped in a story about "lack of self-confidence" and "low self-esteem"? What I heard was that he had been trying, increasingly unsuccessfully, to change her from someone who was suffering from a poor self-image into someone who was proud of herself and her work. It reminded me of a time when I was using an over-the-counter treatment for poison ivy on my leg. I reported to my doctor that the cream wasn't healing the rash, and he replied in a bemused way, "Maybe that's because you don't have poison ivy." He was right, but at first I couldn't believe it. I was the expert on poison ivy, as I had contracted it so often as a child.

So I got to play the doctor and say to Bruce, "Maybe your support isn't working because Alice doesn't lack self-esteem." In the silence that followed I could feel Bruce's bewilderment, the familiar wobbling of certain knowledge. On the theory that Bruce had become a victim of his own narrative, I offered some ideas that would fit a different story, not because I was necessarily enrolled in any of them myself, but as an attempt to break the impasse. "Bruce, perhaps Alice is a perfectionist and wants to be sure she doesn't overprice pieces she herself sees flaws in. Obviously she has a great eye; maybe she doesn't want to show pieces that don't match her standards." And then I threw in some supportive evidence for creating a new story. "Apparently she isn't going to respond to your valiant, ongoing efforts to boost her self-esteem because, as you have already told me, no matter how much others praise her, she is never satisfied."

Then I started making suggestions that would have been a match for an alternate narrative, one in which Alice was seen to be a perfectly self-confident artist who simply found selling distasteful or at best a distraction. "Bruce, what if *you* took over the marketing? You two could form a little business. She could be the talent, and you would be the manager. You could get someone to photograph her work, and then you would make the connections to stores and galleries. You don't even have to let her see how you price the furniture, since it seems she isn't particularly interested in the business of selling anyway." I suggested that he ask her to try this *out of her love for him* (not because there was anything wrong with her), and then I added slyly that he might promise that, in exchange, he would stop badgering her about her self-esteem.

Although this little tale might well have fallen flat, which would be data for building another one, it seems that this new story did indeed replace the old, ill-fitting one. Bruce got right down to forming the business, and Alice, who loved her art, was thoroughly relieved that she didn't have to concern herself with either of the two activities: selling or self-improvement.

Each of their patterns, singularly or in interaction, was standing in the way of a natural flow of events. Bruce was forever the "supporter" to Alice, who showed up regularly as a shrinking violet, though a stubborn one at that. But those were their walking stories. Behind those appearances lay equal strengths of initiative and creativity.

CHAPTER TWELVE

The Power of One

W HEN ORGANIZATIONS REFER TO themselves as "family," as many do, they are generally intending to foster an image of warmth, caring, loyalty, and belonging: all positive qualities. But hidden under the rubric of the word "family," as we all know, are also relationships that are controlling, hierarchical, competitive, neglectful, coercive, or downright smothering. These are the kinds of transactions that are likely to appear in groups or companies when people are unwittingly living out of child stories, no matter how much goodwill is present or how lofty the shared values. So now we can make a new distinction when speaking of an organization: is it the type that is characterized by a culture where people are afraid to express themselves and engage in hidden and polarizing liaisons; or is it the kind that promotes generous, responsible, flexible, and authentic adult points of view?

In the following tale, our heroine, the CEO of a small company, had no notion of how stories create our reality, and no guidebook to help her fix what was going astray in her organization. However, a distressing personal moment of losing control became a disruption that offered a possibility for her own transformation. She found and released what was childish about her perspective that was perhaps triggering similar reactions in others, and the remarkable thing is that her team, under no pressure of orders to do so, followed her lead.

SIBLING-STYLE PARTNERSHIPS

A small, fast-growing design company had more customers than it could handle, yet for all of its success, its profit margins remained slim and cash flow a perpetual issue. When the owners, including the CEO, Patricia McAuliffe, met at the end of the fiscal year to discuss their projections and commitments for the next season, the firm's cofounder and CFO, Cliff Weinstein, was vocal about how burdened he felt. He had taken on all manner of odd jobs that he disliked intensely, tasks that took him away from his real love, designing, and he intimated that all owners must let go of what it was they enjoyed doing in order to focus on keeping the company solvent and growing.

This was not a new conversation for the group, and it was one that habitually provoked feelings of both resentment and guilt in Patricia. Beyond her duties as CEO, designing was her passion as well, and she was on the alert to defend her right to it. She was reluctant to share her pleasure in her craft, as she was convinced the others would think she was getting away with something. "As Cliff one more time put forward the idea that we should all hunker down and become miserable workhorses," Patricia told me, "I snapped at him. I blurted out something like, 'You do what you think you should do, but you don't have to burden everyone else with your unhappiness!'

"A shocked member of our team called out, 'Where did that come from?' I stopped in my tracks. I knew where it came from: I had been more successful than my siblings as a child, and my mother came to downplay my achievements to balance things out between my next younger sister and me. The pattern remains alive and well even now, so much so that when my fiancé and I were about to announce our engagement my mother stopped us, saying, absurdly, that she wanted to 'break the news' to my sister at the right time in private. When Cliff made his suggestion, all I could hear was my mother telling me, in effect, to give up my happiness for others—and I had had enough."

Patricia later reported that after having, perhaps for the first time, so thoroughly violated her own and her family's rules by exploding at Cliff, she had gone into a strange "head trip" over the weekend. "I had a very unpleasant experience of walking around in a deadening fog that I couldn't shake," she said. "I couldn't understand what was happening."

My impulse was to leave our company and never see any of the partners again. I was certain that would suit them anyway. I went through many moments of feeling strangely, almost frighteningly, detached.

But on Sunday morning, while treating myself to a very long shower, a revelation came—thank heavens. The fog I was experiencing was fear! This is all about old family issues, and it feels extremely unsafe—really very treacherous. I realized, too, that of course there was nothing dangerous about the situation in my current job. I was bringing up a memory of another time. I could even remember an incident when I thought my siblings wanted to get rid of me. I noted then that the feelings of jealous siblings can run deep. As I had that thought, almost at the same moment the fog lifted, miraculously, and I came back to my right mind. I laughed and actually said aloud, "Anyway, my colleagues are really nothing like my family."

Patricia told me that she had been aware of the family drama for years, but never before on the emotional, visceral level that she experienced over the previous week, so she hadn't ever been able to put these issues in their place. It was as though those memories had previously been featured in brochure form, sporting phrases about a place she never fully remembered. Now she had actually been to the equivalent of the coast of Italy and back, recognized the differences between this land and that, and knew the topography—the waterways and the rocky promontories of the terrain. Then she flew away from the memory back home to the here and now, and her mind immediately began spinning with ideas for the company. Instead of ruminating about handing in her resignation, she couldn't wait to get back to work.

On Monday morning, Patricia called a partners' meeting. "This is where the real change happened," she said.

In the past, I would have had my back up going into such a meeting. I would have felt defensive. I would have felt frightened. I would have felt guilty. We have had tons of meetings like this and it's been hard for me not to get upset during them. But this time, I felt completely calm. I felt generous and loving toward Cliff and all of my partners. I was able to say, "What do we need to do, so that we are all happy and the company is successful?" It didn't feel like an exchange of my happiness versus Cliff's happiness, but rather a clear-headed, problem-solving place to be. I was able to steer the conversation into a really productive arena and everyone went along with me. I also apologized to Cliff because what he had said the week before appeared so differently to me in this meeting. I told him I was sorry that I had put up such resistance because I now saw that he had only been trying to find ways to support us.

The results were that what I call "the martyr partners," myself included—those people who act as though they must do everything and sacrifice—understood that that is not productive for them or for the company, and all have agreed to bring in outside help. We all saw that it would be more fruitful to have a stellar team around us consisting of a supportive bank (with deeper pockets!), a more involved accountant, and a business consultant. We also raised our prices commensurably and still are receiving more business than we can handle.

Patricia had been generating family dynamics in her company, to the point where she was ready to take her toys and go, and the partners were reacting and perhaps generating them in kind. I cannot overemphasize how common this is and how often it goes unrecognized. In the large corporations where child stories are running rampant across all sectors, from the leadership to people in the most humble positions, claims of "family" can pair with alarmingly ruthless transactions. It took only one person in this little business described here to upgrade the company-wide survival story to produce exceptional results. The new adult story recognized that the competition and the undermining that goes on between siblings is just playground stuff. It feels dangerous to the child, dangerous enough to throw Patricia into a dissociated state, but it is not dangerous anymore for the adult and is easily handled with self-discipline, clarity, and humor. With the aid of the weekend and the warm shower, Patricia was able to bring the memories into consciousness as simply memories, and intervene in the equation she had unconsciously made between those recollections and modern life.

She stepped into an exhilarating feeling of freedom, slipping out of those deferential shoes of hers that had her walking everywhere as a sacrificial victim, and her behavior toward her partners inevitably followed suit. She took on a warm, no-nonsense leadership role and generated a clear space around her that melted away the partners' own fears and confusion such that they also soon found themselves undergoing a transformation or, as we say, they, too, started living as that rare variety of human beings known as true adults. By upgrading a deeply ingrained story, Patricia became an agent of transformation.

CHAPTER THIRTEEN

Can We Change People?
Yes, We Can.

OVER THE YEARS WHEN my partner in our possibility work, Ben Zander, taught his graduate class in music interpretation at the New England Conservatory, I regularly had the opportunity to observe students undergoing a transformation. The level of performance is usually so high at the start that often I could not imagine that there was anything blocking the student's effectiveness. But even at this level, there is always a possibility beyond the magnificence that one is experiencing in the moment.

On one of the Friday afternoons when I was attending the class as a visitor, a vocalist and a trumpet player were performing a piece for voice and solo trumpet. The singer, Jessica, stood stock-still in the middle of a circle made by student chairs, and almost without motion of any kind, as though she were a statue graced by a singing head, started to perform a sublime rendition of "Let the Bright Seraphim" from *Samson*, an oratorio by Handel. Her voice was as clear as mountain lake water, but the solo trumpet easily overwhelmed it. Ben explained that Handel's piece called for the trumpet and the voice to be equal, strong and proud, so he wasn't going to ask the trumpet to pull back. He wanted to find a way for Jessica to release her voice to be everything it could be. Hardly were the words out of his mouth before he was directing the students to draw back their chairs, leaving Jessica standing in a circular area three times its original size.

Ben asked her to begin again, and when her singing got under way he stepped into the circle and drew her by the hand into a dance. At first she resisted, but gradually let go enough to move with the developing rhythm, and before long their feet were gliding around the circle to the music. When Jessica finally became an equal partner in the dance, Ben let her go. She continued to sing and spin on her own with confidence and freedom, such that her voice became now fully a match for the trumpet. She was singing on that razor's edge of sound that musicians long for. The stone that once encased her had cracked wide open. Some of the students were clearly in awe, while others had tears in their eyes.

How many people do you know who would be willing to stand up and twirl while singing in front of their expert classmates? It takes courage to open up so thoroughly and to step so thoroughly beyond the conventions of performance. But there is something more to this story that makes it particularly powerful and moving.

Jessica had been blind from birth.

Jessica's blindness had become more than a handicap for her. It had become the story of her life, and everyone around her was enrolled in it. Every movement of hers told us that her earth was a circle only a few feet wide, and her body was a fortress of stone to support her and keep her upright. Nobody in that room had believed that what they were seeing and hearing was possible, least of all Jessica herself.

Ben was vehement in his conviction that Jessica had to give up living a "blind life" if she was to become a great musician. He took the risk of interrupting the patterns of movement that supported her story, ones that kept her from physically expressing the emotions that are integral to great music: joy, passion, grief, and rapture. He held her firmly in the dance while, within her, different neural pathways grew and made connections, until he could sense that she felt secure enough in herself to take over the new "sighted" patterns of movement, and would be able to continue them, exuberantly on her own.

What allowed Ben to take such risks with her? From the outside, the agent of transformation often looks courageous, or brilliantly strategic, but from the inside it does not seem that way to him at all. For him or her it's all ease and flow. This is because our infinite selves don't put up resistance to the infinite selves of others: they join in collaboration. All resistance arises when our stories clash. So after Ben witnessed Jessica's presentation as a singing head encased in stone, he knew just what to do. He didn't analyze her; he didn't make suggestions about her posture. He swept her into a dance, bringing her into human connection through new ranges of movement and emotion, liberating her from the protective isolation of the story of blindness.

> Yay! I got to dance and twirl and soar! If I can always have that freedom, I will truly be living in a world of possibility.
>
> JESSICA, ON HER CLASS SHEET

Transformation of a walking story can be instantaneous when people are engaged in a shared goal, and when one person puts attention, unencumbered by a child story, on the infinite essence of another person. Unencumbered, in this case, signifies "without an agenda save for the goal of being a medium for others to free themselves up to grow."

The amazing thing is that when you are willing to make the effort to be responsible for how life has been occurring to you and to clear yourself of the bits and pieces of out-of-date narratives — either by simply dropping them or locating them in the context of your development — other people's essential beings will appear before you like magical characters in fairy tales. Then, without thinking, you will know just what to say or do that will allow the frog to become a prince, the Beast a man, and Sleeping Beauty to wake refreshed from a hundred years of slumber.

CHAPTER FOURTEEN

Grow Forever

THOUGH I HAVE BEEN curious about a number of different fields, and have met many magical people who invent and work in them, I haven't yet had the inclination to delve into the mysterious game of football. So when the 2015 season came to a close I was barely conscious that our Boston team, the New England Patriots, had won the NFL's AFC Championship and was on its way to Phoenix to play in the Super Bowl against the Seattle Seahawks. However, as Boston is such a sports-happy town, no amount of resistance on my part saved me from getting caught up in the mania.

I watched the game on a friend's big screen, trying, mostly unsuccessfully, to follow what was going on. It was clear that the two teams were neck and neck throughout the entire game: tied at halftime, Seattle up ten points in the third quarter, and then New England with a gain of fourteen points in the fourth. So as the game lurched to an end, there was a four-point gap between the teams, with the Patriots ahead. But the Seahawks were still in the running. They were down four points but had the ball near the goal line, so there was a good chance for them to score and win. All I could think was, "This is going to finish with one team having a huge loss and one having a tremendous win, but it won't mean anything. These teams seem equally matched." At the very last moment, I got up to get something and missed the critical play. Then it was all over and the Patriots had won. But the networks replayed the intercepted pass that gave the game away often enough so that I got the idea.

In the frenzy of celebration, the coach of the losing Seahawks, Pete Carroll, became the center of every reporter's attention for his spectacular failure, almost rivaling the spotlight on the winning Patriots' coach, Bill Belichick. People were representing Coach Carroll's call to pass at the goal line in such terms as a "catastrophe" for the Seahawks, and a "miracle" for the Patriots. Again, I naively thought, how strange. Someone had to win, so why would we give such dramatic prominence to the last little sliver of play?

"Do you regret that final call?" came the question to Pete Carroll from all sides. "What would you do differently if you had a chance to do it over?" And then relentlessly pressing in, "Have you given yourself time to let go and have a good cry?"

I watched a man who at each question seemed to be trying to translate for the cameras what he experienced into a form that would simultaneously satisfy the interviewers, give a polite nod to the catastrophizers, and also be authentic. He must have known that most people wanted to hear him talk about his anguish; they were eager to find out what he was doing to manage what they assumed was his inevitable feeling of failure, and they were anxious to know how he was assessing himself after making that crucial "mistake." But I didn't see that Pete Carroll was suffering. I didn't see any signs of regret at all. He seemed to me to be so free from fears, self-doubt, and second-guessing that it wasn't easy for him to find the words to answer those double-bound questions. It looked to me as though they simply didn't apply. Carroll delivered a mild correction to one reporter's statement that some people were say-ing it was the worst call in the history of the game. "The worst *result* of a call in the history of the game. If we'd won as we intended, no one would be talking about the call." He almost chuckled.

With only one remaining time-out, and a score of 28–24, Car-roll had decided to err on the side of assuring the most opportuni-ties for the Seahawks to get the ball into the end zone while limiting the chances that the Patriots would have enough time to counter. It didn't work. A rookie named Malcolm Butler stepped in to inter-cept the pass, and the Patriots ran down the clock and won. Carroll had nothing but praise for the young Butler, who had assured the Super Bowl victory for New England.

Watching those interviews, I came to admire Pete Carroll's ma-turity enormously. While he was already using the situation to build the future, he was also very aware of the distress of the mem-bers of his team. So when an interviewer asked him if he had bro-ken down in tears, he said "Yes, once, in the middle of the night," and then in a quiet voice he added, "I was feeling the pain of the team." His middle-of-the-night sleeplessness was prompted not by regret or self-recriminations, but by compassion for the guys and their families. He had to say over and over that personally he didn't spend more than minutes on the loss, he was thinking about the following year, and using the ill-fated event as a tool to plan ahead. Still, it seems that people had a hard time hearing him; I think we can say that in general, it is difficult to understand people who have grown a little further than we have and are occupied with a different set of concerns.

I became very interested in Pete Carroll after those interviews; more so, I have to admit, than I am in the game of football, but these are early days for me. So I read his autobiography and found that, not surprisingly, obtaining self-knowledge has been the bed-rock of his development as a coach. Two events in his life were seminal: Pete Carroll was fired twice from head coaching positions in the NFL, first by the Jets and then by the Patriots. The first dis-missal by the Jets blindsided him. So many extraneous conditions —

undermining by a quarterback, bad-mouthing by a sports talk radio host, a friend's cancer, a firing in Philadelphia, and the snap decision of an owner lying in a beach chair—conspired to create "a perfect storm" that many are still curious about. A precipitous, multifactored trauma of that sort is particularly hard for a person to integrate, and it took the sunny, enthusiastic Pete Carroll some time before he found a story to explain what had happened that put ground under his feet: "In the long run I have to admit that I probably contributed to my firing by the Jets because I didn't do everything I could have done to make sure the owner understood my vision. I didn't understand the scope of my approach well enough to explain it to him in a convincing way." With this statement, Pete Carroll found a way—the adult way—of being able, usefully, to claim responsibility and work on changing a pattern.

Seven years later, Carroll was fired again, this time from his position as head coach of the Patriots, again under very complex circumstances. Among other factors, a shared power structure in the management of the team resulted in the loss of critical players and eventuated in a two-year losing streak. This time Carroll made the assessment that his excitement over being offered the job blocked him from seeing how unwise it was to agree to a position as coach without the authority to make critical decisions about players—a valuable realization. He treated his dismissal from the Patriots from the very outset as an opportunity for self-discovery.

Carroll read widely in psychology and in transformational literature. In search of a vision and mission for his personal life and as a coach, he took the time to look into themes that had remained constant for him over the years as fundamental driving forces and inspiration. He discovered that, from his earliest days, competing had brought him joy and success, and out of that insight came what sounds like a simple, even simplistic philosophy: "Always Compete" and "Win Forever." But it is anything but simplistic. These words translate through Carroll to mean something much more Zen than challenging others to endless duels. He is raising the possibility that you can be clear on your intent to grow and to keep on growing moment by moment; you can greet every engagement as an opportunity to improve on what you have done before, and if you do you are always winning. "The only competition that matters," he says, "is the one that takes place within yourself."

"Always Compete" and "Win Forever" can also be used as a structure within which to observe your patterns and find a new path. Most of us find failure demoralizing—something we would rather not think about. But in the structure of Pete's vision, failure is an inducement to find the pattern or story that took you away from the present moment so thoroughly that you lost your ability to stay in concert with the reality before you.

Supported by his newly developed vision, Pete Carroll turned to the question of the domain that falls to the coach. Notice his questioning approach: "What if my job as a coach is really to prove to these kids how good they already are, how good they could possibly become, and that they are truly capable of high-level performance?" Carroll, it seems, centers on the infinite within his players, and is not fooled by the drama of their war stories or their walking narratives. He maintains a positive, playful, often joyous attitude, bolstered by the freedom of living inside the guidelines of his vision. "Anyone close to me knows I am always looking for the fun in everything I do."

With his vision of Win Forever in place, Carroll then developed and honed three simple rules for his players, rules that are also a structure for transformation, and a support for them to adopt an adult story. These three rules almost guarantee that the person who follows them is saved from the distraction of survival instincts, such as possessiveness, entitlement, and winning over others, and feelings of helplessness, fear, and rage when things don't turn out the way he planned. Here are the three rules:

1. Protect the Team: A perfect instruction to remind a player that he is not, in fact, the center of the universe, and to encourage him in all matters related to the game to adopt and live into a story of contribution.

2. No Negative Talk. No Whining and Complaining: This rule establishes that the game is played in a mode of possibility and not one of survival where players are out for themselves and can be weakened by a victim story. It requires that people be responsible for the effect of their words and their moods, which ensures that the team maintains energy. In addition it fosters feelings of camaraderie and bolsters confidence.

3. Be Early: What powerful little words! What an amazing third rule! The player who lives by "be early" puts himself in charge of his life. It is virtually impossible to be on time, even though people will persistently aim for it, because the time allotted to "on time" is only a split second, whereas being early and being late have eons to play with. If you aim for being on time you will miss and veer to one side or the other and be out of control no matter which side you land on, because you won't be where you intended to be. If you decide to be early, you are always in charge; you will show up as a considerate person as well as a paragon of responsibility.

With the simplicity of his vision and the three rules, Pete Carroll has created ideal frameworks for transformation and growth. The Win Forever philosophy has given him a way of seeing those patterns of his own that lead him to lose connection with the world as it is. This is tremendously important because if he is not continually alert to them as they arise, he loses opportunities to develop teams to the highest level. When you are operating on Carroll's scale, failures tend to be outsized, very public, and numerous. Pete Carroll has been a phenomenal winner throughout his life, but it is to those losing moments that he keeps enthusiastically pointing our attention. Coach Carroll seems to have made a lifelong habit of clearing and rerouting his own patterns, and this has allowed him to create a spectacular team of unburdened players in the Seattle Seahawks. As the years go by, the happiness, joy, unbounded

energy, and strength that come from living a life of ongoing transformation have replaced the energetic boyishness of his youth, and
now illuminate his maturity.

Former Seahawks defensive end Lawrence Jackson shows how
Carroll's philosophy is able to awaken curiosity and admiration in
those not given to thinking in philosophical terms.

"Understanding Coach Carroll, you have to go outside the box,"
Jackson said. "He's not a traditional meathead. He understands life.
He understands how to be successful in life as a person."

CHAPTER FIFTEEN

Resonance

T HERE IS ANOTHER KIND of pattern that is abundant throughout the universe, the sort of pattern that may play a part in our successes as well as what we would call our failures, and is further evidence against naming ourselves "the doers" of our actions. I am now speaking of resonance patterns, the phenomenon described in scientific circles where energy becomes amplified when in proximity to waves of similar tone or length. It's analogous to how movement is initiated when one person persists in speaking up for a future to those who have a will and a desire for what her vision represents, even if that will is latent.

A minor example comes to mind. I think of the time my daughter, Alexandra, invited me to accompany her to an animal shelter to look for a dog for her friend Sarah (she said). I went along, knowing she probably had another design up her sleeve. I had had a border collie for fifteen years and now several years had passed since we buried him, but I was not thinking of getting another dog. At the shelter, a greyhound, looking quite exceptional among other breeds in the dog run, stood still and watched us with an alert and somber air. Alexandra asked the authorities if we might take her out to an enclosure, to get a feel for her. We did, and the two of them played, the dog leaning down on her front paws and feinting movements right and left to invite my daughter into a chase, while I stood by enjoying this merry scene.

An hour later, Alexandra went back to her separate life and I came home with the greyhound. Luna provided me with years of exercise and companionship, and became the delight of my toddler grandson, until at the age of fourteen and a half on a rainy day's run, she streaked along a country road, her body streamlined, her spirit wild, and dropped from a heart attack in midflight.

When I think back to that afternoon at the shelter, I realize that without saying a word, and with no intention on my part, we had instantly formed a band of three resonating beings: one looking to belong, one with canine leanings and a home to support them, and the third with a lively determination to make the connection. Alexandra was clearly the initiator of all that transpired by inviting me to the shelter, but was she the doer? I don't think so; I think we three entered a field of resonance that played out silently into a new configuration for our lives.

THE METAPHOR OF RESONANCE

When you wet your finger and run it around the rim of a wineglass, you create resonance between the vibrations caused by the motion of your finger and the latent vibration rate of the molecules in the glass. At first you may get mere squeaks, but very soon you will hear a tone and as the tone deepens it appears to take on a life of its own, requiring only the lightest touch to maintain its one-pitch sound. This section is about a similar phenomenon in human life. It tells of people in many different fields who have sensed how much resonance there is in society to take on a particular issue. It is about visionary people who have detected the energy—suppressed, hidden, or dormant—that will emerge with an intentional, committed push. Commitment here means dedication to a cause that is beneficial to the whole. It does not mean tenacity in getting one's way that would cause only waves of interference. I've included the minor example of my daughter and our greyhound, because I know she thought it would be good for my health and good glue for the whole family if I had a dog. It wouldn't have been right two years earlier, and she didn't try. But that day, in the dog run, we three fell into an exquisite, if hesitant, attunement, a mutual vibration that gave a "yes" to the initiation of eleven years of devotion.

COMMUNITIES OF COLLABORATORS

Let's posit that there is a spirit in every group or society that is a match for, and resonates with, the self, unbounded and open, that we are able to invent, or perhaps discover, behind our individual walking stories. I imagine a powerful, contributory spirit that is waiting to be recognized, called upon, and set in motion. If we clear ourselves of patterns that block us, listen carefully and speak on key, we may be able to be catalysts for its emergence, like the finger on the glass. The direction of growth in which things want to move may open up for us. And then we will have a community of collaborators, where once we thought there was no hope for change.

These chapters offer five stories of people who by one means or another were able to initiate resonance for their visionary ideas in the world around them. One, a passionate environmentalist, did so by recognizing that the people he thought were blocking him were doing so only within the framework of the stories in his own head. Another, an architect with a gift for relationship, fashioned herself as a tuning fork in front of a group whose energies were all at cross-purposes, with tremendous results. One, a young businessman in a foreign country and an unfamiliar industry, was able to pay exquisite attention to the vibrations in the social fabric and turn a failing company around. Another, an animal rights activist, initiated a transformation of consciousness starting on a local level with very minimal resources. Finally, a group of three separate visionaries previously unknown to one another, one a violinist, one a mother, and the third a speaker/conductor, were able to bring together waves of connection that brought hope to a nation. As a result, each of these enthusiasts, some with no training in leadership, emerged into a resonant field with all elements pointing in the same direction. They provide models for the rest of us, showing that small actions can birth big accomplishments.

CHAPTER SIXTEEN

Things May Not Be as They Appear

SOME YEARS AGO, AN avid environmentalist named John joined a group I was leading that was based on the accomplishment of individual projects brought in by the members. The participants came to know, intimately, that John had a habit of speaking up with fury and passion against commercialism and the misuse of natural resources. During one of the meetings we had yet another opportunity to see it in action. John came in outraged that a developer had just obtained the necessary permits to build a large hotel on a piece of prime property that, if constructed, he said would do irreparable damage to the cliffs and wildlife of his hometown on the south shore of Massachusetts. He had many choice words to share about developers as a breed, as well as bureaucratic town managers, and what he called "your average uncaring citizen." He was planning to storm into a town meeting and challenge people that evening, but he wasn't at all optimistic that he would be able to make any kind of difference. In fact, it seemed that he couldn't wait to confirm for us how hopeless it all was.

A group member, Rachel, suggested it might be helpful to change his story about the cast of characters he was about to meet, but he argued forcefully that it was purely positive thinking to expect anything other than he had described. He presented himself as an expert in dealing with such matters, making it difficult for anyone to contribute a new thought to the dialogue.

When we met next we had no hopes that John had been in any way successful except possibly in rousing up the community against him; but we were wrong. He related that on his drive home, in the privacy of his car, he finally allowed the material that we had been talking about in every session to override his rage. In his own contained space, he had the grace to drop his self-righteousness. He acknowledged to himself that it was really up to him, and him alone, to create plausible stories about the stakeholders of a kind that would enable them all to work together. He thanked Rachel in particular and told us that over the two weeks between our meetings, he reinvented everyone involved in the project to be people who were credibly on his wavelength. And once he had, he went directly to each of them and spoke to them, one by one, as partners.

Here's how he did it: John met with three of the town representatives—whoever was available—and celebrated them as "visionaries" with a tough job to do. The instant look of pride on their faces encouraged him to inquire whether there was any other piece of land that had good views that could be offered to the developer in exchange for the one he was planning to build on. It emerged, miraculously, that there was. Furthermore they agreed to consider making the trade. This gives some indication of how thoroughly John had changed his story. The town reps were no longer people who were resisting him, and they didn't even need "persuading." They appeared to him as folks who at heart shared his goals and who were eager to play under his guidance.

John contacted the developer immediately and introduced the idea of an exchange of properties. He produced an inspiring picture of how this businessman would be seen as a "steward of the environment" through this transaction, a champion of environmental protection. Perhaps it took John longer than most to understand the model of possibility our group was working with because he was a purist who abhorred manipulation of any kind, and combined with his conviction that he had a particularly good grasp of "the truth," he was suspicious of the whole idea of changing your story. But as he drove home after our meeting and ventured into reinterpreting the characters in his hometown, he realized that these alternative characterizations were as true as his negative ones, and probably made for much better connections. He also realized that while there was a purpose to the exercise, it was not for his personal gain, as manipulation implies. When he thought about it, he could see nothing but good coming from his suggestions—positive results for everyone.

Then our once reluctant member-turned-artist went on to paint a picture of the popularity the developer would gain with the townspeople, whom he characterized as "forward looking" and who, by living in this beautiful corner of the world, were showing what they most cared about. As he related the story he radiated such enthusiasm for the community and such confidence in his collaborators, those formerly indifferent citizens, that all those narratives we were holding in our heads about slow-moving bureaucrats and greedy stakeholders simply dissolved. This was a new world!

Last I heard, months after our group disbanded, the properties were switched, there was a new hotel with a great view, and the cliffs remained untouched—except, of course, by wind and sea.

John, the cynic, was after all a passionate person who got sidetracked by a story of hopelessness and tumbled into a sea of negative energy. Perhaps he just couldn't bear the thought of being disappointed again by his fellow man. A mere car drive's shift in his narrative aligned him energetically with the fundamental desires of the community. Now his passion, previously expressed as anger and despair, found resonance in his newly invented world. He initiated a dynamic disruption in the way things were going in his hometown, bringing many elements into happy and heartfelt alignment, and affecting a considerable number of people. Who knows how far the ripples went?

CHAPTER SEVENTEEN

A City at a Crossroads

UNLIKE JOHN, ROB WATSON and his wife, Margaret Howard, had only the most positive outlook on what they would be able
to offer when they flew to Kobe, Japan, on the heels of the January
17, 1995 earthquake. At that time Rob was the senior scientist at
the Natural Resources Defense Council, and Margaret was an
earth-friendly architect.

"We went partly out of a natural desire to do anything we could
to help," Rob said, "and partly because we saw this as a great opportunity to assist the entire city of Kobe to rebuild itself, using new
methods and materials that would maximize the safety of the people and the health of the environment." But they came spectacu-
larly close to missing their window of opportunity altogether.

Rob and Peg had set up an early afternoon meeting with the
major construction companies in the area around Kobe, scheduled

for the day their flight from New York City landed in Japan. At the airport they were detained by a benevolent group of government officials that had gathered to welcome them. "Harassed and jet-lagged, we arrived at our own meeting forty minutes late," Rob explained. "Staring across the table from us were a dozen disgruntled men. Our attempts to start a discussion barely got off the ground, and we could feel their resistance mounting. We understood that we had woefully violated etiquette in arriving so late.

"We hit the right note when we explained that we had been detained by a welcoming committee and were reluctant to dishonor them by leaving prematurely, but we were certainly not fully successful. Heads nodded and the mood lightened to the point where they agreed to converse with us, only to declare vehemently that the people of Kobe would never go for our methods. They then presented a list of possible objections a mile long. With each one," Rob reported, "I edged point by point into an attitude of despair."

Then, suddenly, Peg spoke up brightly, as if she had just alighted from the ether, not a cramped twenty-one-hour flight from New York City. "You may be absolutely right. It may be that none of this will work," she said as she gazed intently at each man seated at the table. And then with a dazzling smile, she declared, "You may be absolutely right, but we'll never know until we try!" She delivered these simple words with electrifying energy, and the response was immediate. "Ah, the Americans!" said a CEO, and the whole table murmured and echoed, "The Americans!"

In a flash, the room metamorphosed into a vigorous force for the reconstruction of Kobe. And then Rob and Peg realized their hosts were way ahead of them. "We couldn't keep up—we didn't have enough of a strategy to propel the initiative forward. We had completely underestimated how far along the business community was in planning for reconstruction. And we underestimated as well the power that an energetic positive attitude—particularly, maybe, because it was couched in terms of a 'we'—would generate."

Later, Rob asked his wife how she did it. "I saw we were all feeding each other's fears," Peg Howard recalled. "You and I were worried about being accepted by them, and they were worried about being accepted by their clients. It was absurd in the most humorous way. And I felt compassion for us all. So I asked myself, 'What's really important here? What's the best thing to do for everyone?' And I knew what we were offering was a pure gift for their society. I felt a burst of joy and strength. I had the energy then to take on everyone's fears, and hold out for our vision."

Lateness, missteps, and the interpretations of disrespect had cast a pall of confusion and darkness over that meeting room in Kobe, and Peg walked in and metaphorically turned on the light. She saw through the walking stories and articulated what was latent behind people's surface irritation. Like the tuning fork that, when struck, starts all other instruments vibrating on the same note, she catalyzed the room into resonance with her offer to help rebuild the city.

From that meeting that began so awkwardly was born the Japanese Green Building Council. As a consequence, a new and highly generative field of interest in sustainability for the built environment was adopted by that very influential culture.

In the next chapter you will read about a businessman whose stated intention was neither to contribute to society nor to improve it. His concern was making a failing business successful. It turns out, however, that when we are walking in an adult story, unafraid of either change or loss, and unconcerned with status and power except as it gives us leverage to do the right thing, we tend to be able to view the way things are with exceptional clarity. Then we are drawn to act decisively, and often end up surrounded by a supportive community resonating with goals and ideas that transcend focus on the bottom line alone.

CHAPTER EIGHTEEN

A Feel for the Times

A YOUNG SWISS MAN, HANSJÖRG Wyss, worked for a fabric company, Burlington Industries, in the late 1950s. Burlington had acquired a little ladies' dress company we'll call Hedblum, which was doing so poorly that the owners of the parent company began to look around for a way to pass the buck for the mistake they'd made in procuring it. They alighted on the solution, never made public, of installing the young Mr. Wyss as CEO to take the rap for Hedblum's imminent failure.

When Hansjörg arrived on the picturesque streets of Boras in western Sweden, knowing nothing about ladies' dresses and not a word of Swedish, he saw immediately the locus of vitality. The newest styles, showcased in the large department stores, were young and vibrant, while Hedblum was still catering to older women through small specialty stores and boutiques. It didn't take him long to see that Hedblum was out of step and on the way out.

Within the first four days, Hansjörg made symbolic moves that called into question long-standing hierarchies that had created rigidity within the organization. The first thing he did was to sell the company car, a Rolls-Royce complete with uniformed chauffeur, the pride of Hedblum. It was used to impress customers arriving at the airport, and it functioned as an emblem of age and established wealth for the company's owner on the town streets. This was a move long overdue, and one that gained most people's respect far more than the sight of the luxury car. Even the somewhat disgruntled owner came around to give his grudging approval when he saw that the new CEO had a positive plan for the company. When on the third or fourth day of his tenure, Hansjörg witnessed a manager punching a time clock, he vowed to free the business from such demeaning practices. This wasn't easy. The organization was resistant to change, and time clocks were a long-established tradition. But through the process of Socratic dialogue in which the managers discovered for themselves that the clocks were inconsequential, he prevailed.

His next move was to inform management that he was going to call a meeting of representatives from the workers and show them the disastrous numbers. "You can't do that," said the managers, and they telephoned headquarters in Basel to prevent him. But Hansjörg did it anyway. He convened a formal meeting with the floor workers and showed them how badly the company was doing. "These are the numbers," he said. "I can't save your jobs unless you help me." The employees were shocked into silence, not only by the truth of the numbers, but because they were not used to being treated as equals, and were certainly not in the habit of expressing their opinions. Finally one woman stood up, and with great presence said simply, "We'll help you," and brought the whole group with her.

"You have to strive to relate on an equal footing with your employees as people, no matter that your roles are different," Hansjörg explained some years later. "Hierarchy in an organization promotes fear and fear is deadly. It kills cooperation and innovation of any kind."

With the workforce on his side, Hansjörg was able to move swiftly and take unusual risks. He decided to channel sales toward the department stores, changing styles appropriately toward a younger look. He discovered that DuPont was making a thinner yarn out of polyester for knitted fabrics that were in line with the new fashion. But Hedblum did not own one machine that could knit—a condition that might well have deterred an older and wiser CEO. Hansjörg, however, discovered a company that built knitting machines that could work with DuPont's yarn, and without consulting anyone, he traveled to Germany to see them. There he made friends with the son of the owner who, he discovered, was having difficulty with his sales department. Accordingly, Hansjörg offered to buy every one of their machines—all in a day and at a very good price, although Hedblum did not have the funds to pay for them. So his next move was to bring together his management in a hotel for the weekend. He told them that Hedblum was about to manufacture a new youthful line of women's clothes called "Jessica of Sweden," and they were also going to start knitting fabrics on the new machines, and selling the new materials, to pay off the sizable purchase. He had no time to hire new managers, so he knew he had to convince everyone in that room of the wisdom of the new strategy. Just as he had done with the workers, Hansjörg made it clear that he wanted and needed the managers' help. No doubt because they had seen that their young and visionary CEO had his finger on the pulse of the market, and had put such effort and energy into creating a collaborative community, from the shop floor to the highest echelons of management, they all stepped up. "I never went for maximum profit," he said in reflecting back on his experience over his lifetime. "I always went for maximum cooperation."

Jessica of Sweden became a popular brand, sales of dresses and fabrics multiplied, and Hedblum flourished. In the meantime, Hansjörg, who had kept his eye on the fabric market, determined that the cotton industry was about to introduce drip-dry cottons and surge ahead of the demand for synthetic fabrics. Unwilling to take on that next challenge in a country he was only visiting, and in an industry that was not his choice, he moved on after only two years, leaving Hedblum at the top of its game, in the black and in the pink.

Like others described in these pages, Hansjörg Wyss was never known to be held back by any of the universal walking stories that cripple so many enterprises: the story that one person can't make a difference, the story that change is difficult and there is virtue in leaving things the way they are, as well as the story that position is important and that people in high places should be treated with deference solely because they are at the top. That allowed him to be clear-eyed and alert to the way the world was moving; and because he was carrying no story that his survival was at stake, he was not afraid to take some quite dazzling risks. It also helped that he wasn't looking for personal trappings of success. His passion was management, pure and simple.

TRANSFORMATION

By reducing hierarchies through strong personal relationships, the young Mr. Wyss was quite consciously moving into resonance with his employees and his managers, as well as the German company that made knitting machines. He acted decisively without waiting for approval because he knew that his moves would create the conditions necessary for future alignment no matter how resistant to change people were. In a matter of a few months Hedblum was transformed into a flexible and nimble organization that was able to move with the times.

Some years later, Hansjörg went on to develop one of the world's largest medical device companies, Synthes, with offices in Switzerland and the United States. His recipe for success was keeping the organization flat and simple as long as he could. He says it was most important that he stayed in touch with what was going on inside the company as it was expanding. "If you lose touch," he says, "it may take awhile, but eventually the company will fail." He was famous for hanging out on the shop floor, talking with the employees. "One of the reasons it is critical to be familiar with what's happening is because as soon as you come out with one product you have to be deeply immersed in producing the next one. The next wave is already on its way."

Hansjörg sold his company at just the right time, as you might imagine, and through his charity and his advocacy, legions of impoverished women and children found the help they needed, payday loans were abolished in many states across America, great swaths of wilderness were protected, art museums were enriched, and teams of researchers in new technologies were supported to produce for mankind at levels they never dreamed of.

The lesson here is that if you open your eyes and heart and assume you can see what wants to happen, you will very likely fall into deep resonance with the world around you, so you will be able to see how things are moving into the future. You will know when to act swiftly and when to bide your time, and it won't be a personal thing—you will be a translator and a transducer of the rhythms of the world at large. You don't waste time in meetings that produce no results, but you may spend half a day helping the son of an employee think out his future, or visiting a friend's mother in the hospital. You prefer the tram to a limousine, because you stay in touch with people that way, and you exhibit a lifestyle that connects you to the heartbeat of the community, not to the few within it who are very rich. You are always on the lookout for the next mountain to climb, which in Hansjörg's case was often a physical one. He has scaled a good portion of the world's most challenging peaks, short of Everest, and for that you have to be very aware and in tune.

CHAPTER NINETEEN

Farm Animal Utopia

THIS IS A STORY of a very large vision that took root in a hard up area in what some might call the middle of nowhere, USA. The heroine of our tale, Daniella, was supported from her earliest days by a story in which she saw herself as a strong partner in every project she undertook, of which there were many. She began volunteering in animal shelters at the age of twelve. As she grew older, she joined the animal rights movement and spent many of her weekends in a human chain of protesters, barring people from entering fur salons and vivisection labs. "It was a really empowering time for me," she said with a hint of nostalgia. "It was wonderful to be in such a group of like-minded people, all doing what we felt was the right thing; the thing we had to do. We were arrested time and time again, but because of our numbers, and maybe our spirit as well" — she laughed — "the police always let us off."

When, a few years later, she took a job in a special education setting supporting foster children, Daniella drew on the strength she had gained from her experience with civil disobedience. She had learned that she wasn't afraid to stand up to anything: she had become an old hand at saying a definitive "no." By far the most difficult part for her of working with problematic, acting-out children wasn't communication or discipline; it was witnessing widespread institutional abuse, because of either bureaucracy or ignorance. She gives the following example. She and another worker had been visiting a thirteen-year-old autistic boy in foster care twice a week with the understanding that he would get continuous oversight. He was big for his age and very strong, and his foster family depended on the services Daniella offered to help them handle him. Two years into the boy's placement, the state cut back on funds and the agency insisted that Daniella stop visiting the boy and his family. The foster family was unable to manage him without the agency's support, prompting the supervisor to order Daniella to drop this now bonded autistic child at a hospital, indicating that it was the end of their responsibility. Daniella stood her sturdy ground and refused to be the abandoner, forcing the supervisor to deliver the boy herself.

Subsequently, Daniella asked for a meeting with the board of the nonprofit that had hired her, and spoke out loudly and clearly about how harmful it is to ignore children's needs for attachment. She also resigned then and there. The power of Daniella's visionary clarity had its effect. Two years later, the board came to her and apologized, having instituted most of the changes she had recommended.

Out of a job at twenty-two, Daniella took some time to turn inward and search for her true calling. "As much as I cared about children, it always came back to animals," she said. "I developed a dream of a world where people would see and understand animals in their full potential as emotional creatures, developed and aware, and people would treat them with respect and love. But my dream went further than that. It began to shape into an idea that animals could be with people as animals really are—smarter and more sophisticated than most people think—and people could be with animals as people really are, not as exploiters but as compassionate beings. I wanted to be able to provide the conditions for that relationship to take place, and cause a shift in consciousness." These ideas began to formulate in her mind as a movement that could go far. To Daniella, the transformation of our human relationship with animals into one of kindness and deep respect was almost a condition for the viability of our life on earth.

Daniella settled on the idea of a farmed animal rescue and sanctuary as the practical vehicle for bringing her dream into reality. In order to understand best practices and become familiar with the variety of services already in existence, she took a job for a year transporting abused and sick animals to shelters up and down the eastern seaboard.

Then, at twenty-three, she was ready to take a risk. With only her very small savings, she went looking for land that was suitable and affordable. She decided to restrict her search to the East Coast of the United States, within driving distance of her aged grandmother in Boston. So she opened up a map of New England on the floor, stood above it and tossed down a handful of pennies, having decided that she would visit each area where a penny landed. In each place she would look for terrain that would be appropriate for a start-up farm and seek out property to buy or lease.

Daniella toured Massachusetts, Vermont, and New Hampshire, visiting the spots selected by her coin toss. At last she came to a little town called Penobscot on the coast of Maine, and there, at the exact place where one penny had come to rest, she found seven acres of land at the right price to begin her mission.

From participating in so many protests, Daniella said, she learned an important lesson in how to bring about change. Getting a conversation going was the critical factor, introducing people to issues they may never have thought about, and giving them a starting point for talking. From that awareness, Daniella discovered her staying power: that it is wise to start small and set up systems in mindful ways. If you rush to the goal, you'll lose information. "Don't expect things to come right away," she said. "Have patience."

Fifteen years later, after much patience on all sides, Peace Ridge Sanctuary has rescued more than three thousand farmed animals from neglect and abuse and provided them with medical care and a healing environment, all on donations from people who resonate with Daniella's well-articulated vision. "This is a year and moment in time I've been waiting for all my life. You know when you've made it, everything aligns!" said Daniella. At the time of her speaking, Peace Ridge Sanctuary was in transition to a larger property that would serve the animals' needs for serenity and increased space, while allowing more people to visit. Daniella doesn't want to expand the number of lifetime animals they support on the farm, animals they care for over the duration of their lives—currently about two hundred—but she does want to extend the farm's mission. She wants to demonstrate to the public how it can be done, and mentor others in starting sanctuaries of their own.

Most of all, she wants to showcase a place where people can feel peaceful and find resonance with animals in their peaceful state. She wants people to see, for instance, how a goose whose mate was shot finds comfort in Daniella's lap, its head nestled under her arm, how loyal cows can be to one another, and how a particular rooster takes care of his blind companion by day, and roosts next to her at night, covering her with his wing.

Peace Ridge Sanctuary offers education for adults and school-children, mentors families that are adopting dogs from its dog and cat adoption service, and is the go-to place for people in the area who suspect that animals are being abused. It is also a beacon of hope for animal lovers that there can be a better way, and it is being demonstrated before their very eyes. Although Peace Ridge is unable to shelter every referral, it is dedicated to finding a solution for every call regarding an animal in need.

Daniella is immersed in ideas of resonance. She maintains an attitude that if you believe in something, having faith that something will work will make it work, and because her vision and its articulation bring out similar energies in others, it usually does. "People generally don't understand what we are doing, but if they come in contact with it they will support it," she said with joyful conviction. Daniella is like a vibrating musical instrument that brings others into harmony. How else could this shoestring operation have thrived?

There are several things we can take away from the story of Peace Ridge. First, it demonstrates that achieving informed clarity about what *you* want that is in tune with what we surmise all people want in an abundant world is key to creating resonance patterns. Another thing we see is that if we took the time and were not blocked by child stories, each of us could come to know the specific pattern of our individual contribution. In addition, Daniella shows us that staying open, having patience, and starting a global conversation at the local level—aligning with the rhythm of things—helps gather a resonant community. Daniella reveals, as do many of the other characters in this section, that you don't have to be born with resources or privilege to make a contribution to the world and live a connected, emotionally rich life. She demonstrates that if you walk with confidence and passion, abundance will very likely show up around you.

CHAPTER TWENTY

Puebla and Beyond

I N THE FOLLOWING TALE, huge resonant forces came together through the will of many people: a will that had long been
repressed with no apparent opportunity for change. It started in a
small classroom in Mexico, initiating a metamorphosis that spread
out and touched parts of the whole country. It is dramatic corrobo-
ration of how a nation can exhibit a walking story of intractable
despair, while underneath and out of sight are buried impulses of
passion and hope ready to spring into action when a metaphorical
finger finally makes contact with the vibrations on the rim of the
glass.

One of the heroes of this story is a man named Julio who had
left Mexico to continue his studies on the violin in Switzerland
and spent eleven years playing in the Suisse Romande orchestra
in Basel. Then, disillusioned with the itinerant life of an orches-

tral musician, he returned to Puebla with the intention of building a music program for children on the model of El Sistema, the
highly successful, publicly funded program in Venezuela initiated by conductor/politician José Antonio Abreu, with the mission to lift kids out of poverty through classical music.

The belief of the El Sistema movement, centered in a philosophy of human dignity, is that every child, rich or poor, can learn to
experience and express great music deeply. For Dr. Abreu and his
followers, the way out of poverty lies in strengthening the spirit
through a music education based in love and joy in an aspiring,
nurturing community. To run a program like this in Mexico was
Julio's dream.

So on his return from Switzerland, Julio visited all the schools
in the area, auditioning children for their musical talent, giving ear
tests and rhythm tests to more than eight hundred kids. Then, by
soliciting donations of instruments and securing a small rehearsal
space, he built his own program of thirty children. But it wasn't
long before Julio started suffering from a lack of resources and
faintness of heart and succumbed to the story of hopelessness. He
just couldn't see where it would go from there.

A woman named Lenore, the mother of two of the youngsters
in Julio's band, wanted desperately for her children to have the
opportunities that she foresaw as the future of his program. In support of this, Lenore volunteered at a big conference in Puebla,
Ciudad de las Ideas, that seemed to promise her access to people
with resources of many kinds. When she saw that a conductor
named Benjamin Zander was on the docket, she volunteered to
be his guide throughout the conference. Lenore had done her
homework on her guest, and during the drive to Puebla from the
airport enrolled Ben in the idea of bringing some new inspiration
to Julio.

The next morning Lenore drove by the hotel to take the mae-
stro to the small town on the outskirts of Puebla where Julio had
his little school. Just as they were leaving, Ben caught sight of a
man he had met at the dinner the night before, who was making a

documentary on the conference for Spanish TV. In the spirit of the moment, he called out, "Eduardo, come with us! This will make a great episode in your documentary." So in the same spirit of spontaneity Eduardo gathered together the four on his team and piled into the SUV. The seven people, with cameras and sound equipment, drove forty-five minutes to a run-down, very poor section of a neighboring suburb.

Inside a small hut that served as the music school, Julio gave a little speech welcoming everyone into the overflowing space that included the little orchestra and the parents of the children, as well as the seven from the SUV. Then he raised his baton with determined cheerfulness to start the "concert." For all Julio's efforts, the children sat grim-faced, sawing out a truly monotonous version of "Twinkle, Twinkle, Little Star" from volume one of the Suzuki method. What an incongruity there was between the sounds of kids struggling with the excruciating beginning stages of learning string instruments and the formidable presence of the international TV crew.

The children played to the very end without expression, but as the last tuneless notes faded away, something completely unexpected happened. The visiting conductor got up and began to clap wildly, exaggeratedly, really outlandishly, infusing huge energy into the room. The children viewed this wild stranger with astonishment from their positions hunkered down in their chairs. For a moment there was silence, then Ben sprang into action.

He got the violins and two violas on their feet, exhorting the cellos to imagine they were standing up as well. Taking the baton from Julio (who was only too happy to offer the kids a new experience and, personally, to be infused with energy once more), Ben started them again on "Twinkle, Twinkle." The volume of their sound swelled under this bizarrely energetic conductor. Then he asked a question that made it impossible for the kids to keep straight faces: "Listen closely, this is going to be hard. Can you play your instrument and *smile* at the same time?" Repressing giggles, they played the next few bars. The strange visitor again exhibited over-the-top excitement, clapping riotously. "Now," he said, "I'm going to ask you to do something really difficult. It's like patting your head and rubbing your stomach, which is very difficult, see?" He made an exaggerated demonstration. "Now I want you to play your instrument and smile and *walk* at the same time. Do you think you can do that? (Sorry, cellos.)" Almost deliriously, the children nodded.

As Julio joined in on his own violin, Ben increased the tempo significantly to match their walking rhythm and led them around the room, skipping and bending, bobbing and dipping. He had some children playing one rhythm and others another. All at once, they were performing "Twinkle, Twinkle, Little Star" exuberantly, energetically, and at quite a satisfying tempo, and had no trouble whatsoever keeping smiles on their faces. As the cameras whirred, some of the parents started dancing in the crowded space, while others listened with rapt attention to their bright-eyed, sophisticated children who were all of a sudden *playing music*.

A MOVEMENT WAITING TO HAPPEN

Hearing the story at the conference dinner that night, Ricardo Salinas, the owner of Mexico's leading television conglomerate, gave Ben his card with a private number on it with instructions to tell Lenore that if they aired the film on TV in Spain, she should bring him a copy. Sure enough, the episode with Julio was shown on Spanish TV, and Lenore promptly got in touch with Ricardo Salinas.

In anticipation of this moment, Lenore had cleverly put together a ten-minute clip from a film of El Sistema of Venezuela that Julio had in his possession. She played both videos for Ricardo Salinas. He was deeply moved by what he saw, realizing at once the implications for social justice for disadvantaged children. On the spot, he offered to fund Julio's program in full and, in addition, he acted on his newly formed vision and insisted on funding a similar program in every one of the thirty-one states in Mexico!

Then, using his considerable influence, he persuaded local authorities as well as the federal government to join him in setting up youth orchestras all over the country. This was very much facilitated by Julio who, having already identified 800 promising kids, put out a notice for 250 more. Six hundred children, who had had no musical education, but an unbounded desire to participate, arrived to audition. With Ricardo Salinas's help, Julio quickly got instruments into their hands and teachers to teach them.

AN AUDIENCE OF TEN THOUSAND

Ricardo Salinas wasted no time raising the ante and provided funding for a concert, to take place in November in Mexico City, three years after the incident in Puebla. Starting the prior June, the teachers and kids rehearsed all summer from ten in the morning till six in the evening. And when school started, they kept the momentum going by doing their homework on the bus, and rehearsing from four to eight at night, for a total of 126 rehearsals. Lenore called Ben to come down to Mexico to see what had emerged from their initiative. What he saw staggered him: ten thousand people were crowded into a huge concert hall in Mexico City to hear this first youth concert. An orchestra of 186 and a choir of over 200 performed selections from Beethoven's Ninth Symphony, Orff's *Carmina Burana*, *Danzón No. 2* by Márquez, and among other pieces, a trumpet concerto performed by an eight-year-old. The playing was simply amazing. Tears were flowing all around as children who three years before had never played a note on an instrument poured their hearts and souls into the music with remarkable skill. The audience responded with one standing ovation after another as the kids, trained to be open to acknowledgment, stood confidently, proudly, with huge grins on their faces. Taking his bows and leading the whole extravaganza was Julio, who had realized his dream.

Within thirty-six months, twenty-three orchestras sprang up and fifty were planned for the upcoming year. Julio's bands acquired their own building in Puebla, a disused factory that has been converted to a rehearsal space. By the three-year mark the youth orchestra initiative had become a huge political force in Mexico. Julio is the conductor of a national movement involving tens of thousands of kids, along with their siblings, parents, and grandparents, with no end in sight.

The orchestra movement in Mexico is an example of "something wanting to happen," or perhaps "waiting to be ignited." It wasn't that people weren't working hard prior to our scene in the little building in Puebla. Many parents were making big sacrifices to bring their children to Julio—one parent was driving three hours a day so his child could be in Julio's orchestra. However, a universal story that it is impossible to make big changes had had a firm grip on that community, and it showed up in the listlessness of the children and in Julio's depression.

Lenore was neither a conductor nor a famous person with connections but she was in possession of a greater power: she walked, talked, and dreamed the story of possibility. Her eyes open for opportunity, she volunteered to deliver Ben, a man noted for his ability to rouse passion and animate communities, to the conference and so to Julio. As she hoped he would, Ben provided a blast of white heat that incinerated the mountain of scarcity thinking and despair in Julio's little classroom and increased the tempo of change. He lit a fire of joy in the hearts of the players, the cameramen, and the relatives, and Lenore and Ricardo delivered it through the media to all of Mexico. The brilliant Lenore and the visionary Julio stayed active on the ground to do the work and make the vital connections that quickly allowed Ben's flash of disruption to result in a far-reaching community of thousands of collaborators, resonating with Julio's and Lenore's vision.

WAVES OF CONNECTION

Resonance has been the subject of this section, the alignment and amplification of waves of energy that are a vibrant feature of the universe at large. Each of the characters in these stories has sought to tune in and increase resonance in order to experience connection with others and gather resources as a team. They do it by articulating what they want to see happen, clearly, and without equivocation. They speak to the loving authentic self, the self of possibility masked by the walking story. They speak to the human being within who, assured of safety, is naturally cooperative. We saw examples of this in John's reinterpretation of the various citizens of his town on the south shore, and in Peg's warm, enthusiastic words to the seemingly reluctant Kobe businessmen. They create resonance by sharing information about the subject of their vision, whether it be the story behind the music, or the true nature of domesticated animals, or the bad news about the numbers in a company, so that everyone can be on the same page. They create resonance by watching the tempo of change and leading others into the rhythm, whether it means slowing things down, as at the animal sanctuary, or speeding things up, as in Sweden or in Mexico. Finally, each of the protagonists has formed himself into a pure oscillating crystal, living in an adult story, transmitting its purpose into the world.

PART III

You in

Partnership

Implicit in the last section is that everything is vibrating; the whole of the universe is oscillating at specific and varying frequencies. At times we feel we are out of sync, that nothing is going right, that we are running into interference patterns at every turn. At other times we have the expansive, empowering feeling that we are in flow. In those moments, our ideas and our physical bodies are somehow in resonance with everything: with those close to us, and even with those across the globe in our virtual communities. The actors in chapters 11 through 20 displayed a developed ability to amplify such resonance and move forward as a team.

So far I have made the suggestion that our child parts, with their egocentric stories, create patterns of interference that block us from making authentic relationships and hinder us from being fulfilled and effective. Now it may be the moment in our journey to grow up another notch by stepping a little farther away from that sweet spot in the center of the universe: the place where we got to be important and right and able to blame everyone and everything else for what went wrong. If we gain more of an overview of the miraculous way in which things evolve and work, we may even *create a new story and a new adult worldview that will reflect how we fit into a much larger patterned system. We might end up in a new narrative, in which we are most responsible when we claim we are not the doers of our actions at all. How can that be? Let's widen the frame to see.*

CHAPTER TWENTY-ONE

Expanding the Frame

THERE ARE PEOPLE WHO claim they can always find a parking space wherever they go. My friend Luis is one of them. He says that most people are looking for actual parking spaces, but he looks for the flow of things. He scans the scene and asks himself questions such as "How purposeful is that pedestrian, and where will his walking take him? Is his hand moving into his pocket for his keys? If many people on the street are traveling in the same direction, perhaps some event has just let out and they will be going to their cars." He says his ability to find a parking space is related to his skill as a classroom teacher. He has to grasp what is going on over the whole room, and he has to anticipate the kids' next moves before they happen. So when Luis wants to park he automatically thinks, "Where is my parking space, the one that will open up soon?" And he widens his field of vision.

STRADDLING THREE WORLDVIEWS

I had an experience some years ago that caused my mind to open up to see one event from three quite different vantage points. While attending a meeting across town, I got an emergency call from an acquaintance who lived on my street. "A tree of yours has fallen," she said. My mind went into shock. "A big tree?" I asked from some distant consciousness. "THE tree?" She said it was a big one but she didn't know whether it was THE one. People were worried that I might have been struck by it, so she was glad to have found me.

I raced home, holding on to the thin thread of hope that it might not have been the gigantic silver maple that was the focal point of my house, yard, and soul. But as I neared my street, I came upon a policeman rerouting traffic and I could see beyond him that it was, its body lying across the road. "The road is blocked off," he said nicely, "take Highland Street."

"But," I said, "that's my tree," tears now spilling over.

"Do you live here?" he asked.

"Yes," I said desperately, "that's my tree (or sister or uncle). I have to get through!" And he let me pass.

With an enormous crack, the tree had split under the force of a freak funnel of wind, all one hundred feet of it going into free fall, clipping off a corner of my porch roof and landing cheek by jowl alongside the house, from where it extended across the street and down the side street. I was devastated. I climbed onto its enormous trunk at the source and lay facedown, stretched out far above the ground, and wept.

Below me, my next-door neighbor was asking me whether I had insurance to cover her crushed peonies. Someone said how lucky I was that it didn't smash straight through the house. The neighbor who lived directly behind me, a Senegalese shaman, appeared out of the shadows below where I lay. He told me in a soft voice that he had heard the mighty crack and had gone to his window. He saw the tree start to fall straight toward the center of my house, and he said he prayed that it would turn, and as he prayed he saw it twist to the left and just miss the house and crash to the ground with a roar that shook the neighborhood. I clutched the huge bole of my tree. A little later a man in a hard hat approached and looked up at me. "Madam," he said in a kindly way, "there are wires hanging everywhere. It isn't safe for you to stay where you are. The city has to cut up and remove the trunk of the tree and take down the other half. It's not stable."

So after a few more moments, and very reluctantly, I peeled myself off the body of my ancient and beloved friend and I expressed my gratitude to the tree for sparing the house in its fall, having no doubt in my mind that it did so because of the love we bore each other.

Later in the afternoon, I watched as a tree specialist, suspended near the top of the smaller standing half of the tree, cut it down piece by piece. He called down to me. "You know why the main trunk didn't hit your house? The grain of the wood is twisted. It must have spiraled to the left as it fell."

Three points of view as to why my house was spared: the power of prayer, the strength of love, and the observations of science. No doubt the scientific explanation will satisfy most readers, with prayer as a distant second. Love will probably get no shrift, except from me. But I ask, "Why limit yourself to the physical evidence found in the solid wood? Why not expand the frame, and your mind as well, to include other powers that may have tipped the balance?"

INTERCESSORY POWER

There have been many scientific studies to test the power of the mind, or minds, to intercede on behalf of others. Because such a notion violates the dominant paradigm of the day, even highly controlled studies, the results of which would be thought convincing enough in another field, are easily dismissed. One assay, the Cha-Wirth-Lobo study, has provoked a storm of criticism. This study involved 219 women ages twenty-six to forty-six, who received in vitro fertilization treatment over a four-month period at Cha General Hospital in Seoul, South Korea, in 2001. The women were randomly assigned to one of two groups: a group that would receive intercessory prayer (prayer focused on benefiting another) and a control group. The people praying were in the United States, Canada, and Australia, halfway around the world from the women for whom they prayed.

None of the women seeking fertility treatment nor anyone involved with their care was informed that the study was occurring, and it was claimed that there were double and triple security measures imposed to ensure anonymity of the data. The people praying were practiced in distance healing but were not necessarily associated with a particular religion or a belief in God.

The results, published in *The Journal of Reproductive Medicine*, showed that women who were on the receiving end of the prayer were almost twice as successful in becoming pregnant as the women who hadn't received that focused attention, 50 percent versus 26 percent.

News of the study was picked up and scattered throughout the popular press here in the United States and in turn received a riot of indignation from the medical profession criticizing the methodology, decrying the journal that had published the findings, but mainly citing the unreliability of the authors, one of whom had served a five-year prison term for fraud on another matter. I could find no one who disclaimed the numbers—probably because pregnancy is one of those irrefutable findings: either you are or you aren't.

KEEPING THE MIND OPEN IS NOT EASY

"Reality" is ultimately a belief system, no matter how sure we are that the way we see things is the way they really are. Our own reality is like a Geiger counter, beeping frantically as we bump into ideas and claims that violate it. But let's stretch our minds a little, let's widen the frame of what we consider possible. *Possible*, not "true."

For instance, we quite rightly and fairly imagine that among earth's phenomena, things vary extensively in terms of activity levels. We recognize that there are nonmoving objects like rocks and chairs (when nobody repositions them), and slow-changing objects like trees and ice caps, and things spinning at high speed like six-year-old boys and Jack Russell terriers, and variations in between. But those may be just surface impressions that facilitate our ability to navigate through our physical world. If we could look through appearances and view things on a much smaller scale, we would see that everything is dynamic; every part of everything is making connections, reacting, and changing. Rocks are "communicating," as are trees, chairs, little boys, and turbocharged dogs. Consider this, from a 2007 *New York Times* article by essayist and philosopher Jim Holt:

"Take that rock over there. . . . It consists of an unimaginable number of atoms . . . all jiggling around at a rate that even our fastest supercomputer might envy. And they are not jiggling at random. The rock's innards 'see' the entire universe [using] the gravitational and electromagnetic signals it is continuously receiving."

Holt goes on to say that the process within the rock parallels any series of mental states our own brains might perform. Cognitive scientist David Chalmers echoes the idea that consciousness is fundamental and perhaps universal in his 2014 TED Talk. "Wherever there is information processing," he says, "there is consciousness."

On a similar note, Suzanne Simard, a dedicated forest ecologist at the University of British Columbia, and her colleagues discovered that trees and plants really do communicate and interact with one another.

Simard uncovered the existence of an underground web of fungi wrapping around and connecting the trees and plants of some vast ecosystems. The symbiotic relationship between plants and fungi enables the purposeful sharing of resources, helping the whole system of trees and plants to flourish and giving it resilience against the attack of fire or disease. The largest trees, the "mother trees," appear to function as hubs, sending information via the network of fungi and smaller plants to the trees on the outermost edges of the forest.

Let your mind, that neural network, imagine for a moment that we are part of a greater network, an ecosystem into which new members are continually welcomed and integrated, forming increasingly complex patterns, combining and recombining into new arrangements of wholeness and balance. Imagine further that every seed, every newborn child, every organization, every bird, every galaxy, and every part of every galaxy is evolving to fulfill and elaborate this design.

As we have noted, nothing duplicates what went before, and nothing will ever, *ever* happen again, no matter that our minds, in their attempt to simplify, insist that life repeats itself. How often do we say, "The same thing happened last year," or "I can't believe I fell into that same trap"? But as Heraclitus said 2,500 years ago, "No man ever steps in the same river twice, for it's not the same river and he's not the same man."

This is not to say that the universe's activity is random. There seems to be an overarching context around it all, a principle of self-organizing emerging systems. It appears that the wider we extend our frame, the more we understand how deeply patterned is the universe.

Take the seemingly random actions of butterflies, for instance. When we expand the frame and take a broader view, we see that an individual butterfly's behavior is an element of a long, overarching pattern, spanning generations.

As spring temperatures rise, the adult monarchs come out of hibernation and leave the oyamel fir tree forests of Mexico to start their northward journey to the northeastern United States in search of the milkweed plant that hosts their larvae. But they don't get far before they land, breed in the southern United States, and die. The second generation continues northward, once again on the lookout for milkweed plants where they can reproduce. The cycle repeats for another couple of generations before the temperature drops, and fall returns, and the more than two-thousand-mile southward migration begins. Amazingly, even though several generations have passed, monarchs return to the same forests, even the same tree, as their ancestors.

Certainly, along that journey, individual butterflies become attracted to particular flowers and trace unique flight patterns, and appear to have minds of their own. No two butterflies sport the same markings, or go to the same places overall, or sip nectar from the same sequence of flowers. If you were to restrict your view to the life of one butterfly, you would never see the larger pattern. You would be certain that none of those who start out would ever wind up back in the forest of their origins, and you would be right. But if you limited the scope of your vision, you would miss the miracle of miracles: that their great-grandchildren do.

I'm a big fan of inquiring as to what lies outside the frame of our view in almost every case. Remember how our image of that messy, lazy, impossible-to-manage secretary transformed when we pulled back the curtain a bit? Widening the frame teaches us how little we know, and it can often give us access to experience that has not yet been organized into "what we know" by our upper brain, sparking the delicious sensation of being fully alive.

We conduct our lives as if "closed systems" were possible, treating a broken arm in isolation, without anticipating the effect on the rest of the body or the effect on the family of such incapacity. We assume that healthy weight is up to the individual and blame ourselves when we fail, not taking into account the bombardment of advertising for addictive foods we receive. Yet there *are* no closed systems in nature, no matter that it is so much more convenient to deal with limited facts. Although we may get enough of the facts to be effective, we will never, ever get the whole story about butterflies or secretaries or broken limbs, or weight gain. However, the more we open our eyes to how things are working within and around us on different scales, the more likely we will get the chance to participate with the evolution in progress, and just maybe, like the blind singer Jessica, take steps to dance with it all.

A Fractal Universe

There is another form of ubiquitous patterning that emerged fully into public consciousness late in the twentieth century, although it had been staring us in the face from the beginning of time. Have you ever found yourself mesmerized by the patterns of ice forming on a windowpane, for instance, and noticed the similarity between the intricate frozen images and the organic shapes of ferns and flowers? You wouldn't have been the first to do so.*

This is an indication that we live in a "fractal" universe, a universe where fundamental shapes and processes can be found on all scales, from infinitely large to infinitely small. Think of a tree; if you break off a branch and stick it in the ground, it looks like a smaller tree, and if you snap off a twig and put it in a bit of earth outside a dollhouse, well, it looks remarkably like a doll-sized tree. We have learned that our moon orbits the earth the same way the planets in our solar system revolve around our sun, the way the sun traces a path around the center of the galaxy. Fractals! Each set of objects is different but exhibits the same type of structure from whatever scale you are observing it. Human babies emerge from their fractal mothers, just as baby mice are fractal iterations of theirs. Look at a coastline from a hillside and then from a plane at thirty thousand feet and, though you're able to see so much more of it from that distance, the jagged edges will sport a remarkably similar pattern. Lie on your back on the ground and look at the

---

* See chapter 25 for a description of ice crystals on a windowpane in the song "The Dream of Spring" (*Frühlingstraum*), part of the *Winterreise* song cycle by Schubert.

edges of the clouds against the sky: the small bits look just like the larger bits.

Since 1975, when the Polish-French mathematician Benoit Mandelbrot created a geometry of fractals to show that things typically considered to be messy, rough, or chaotic were actually ordered in how they develop and proliferate, the field has exploded. By running Mandelbrot's simple equation, computers can grow emergent, gorgeous patterns, into infinity, that display both self-similarity and uniqueness.* Fractal structures keep appearing wherever we look—for example, in the way our fingers relate to our hands, in the way organizations grow, in J. S. Bach's cello suites,[†] throughout the arts and architecture, in plants and blood vessels— all the way out to clusters of galaxies and all the way in to DNA. Researchers have recently discovered that even the genome is structured as a fractal, where small pieces of DNA fold into "globs" and those globs fold into larger globs that are organized in such a way that they maintain the same pattern as far in or as far out as you go.[‡]

The late Oliver Sacks, the popular science writer and professor of neurology at New York University School of Medicine, discovered that the geometric patterns in migraine hallucinations appear in nonliving things as well—" 'in the formation of snow crystals, in the roiling and eddies of turbulent water, in certain oscillating chemical reactions'—allowing us 'to experience in ourselves not only a universal of neural functioning but a universal of nature itself.' "[§]

---

* The reason why fractal mathematics are so pervasive in our universe is that the universe was formed in rotation, and over time broke up into rotating eddies on successively smaller scales producing self-similar structure throughout, in line with fractal mathematics. It is no accident that human DNA preserves this vorticity, or spin geometry, which allows our intimate being to be in resonance with cosmic structures of all sizes, animal, vegetable, and mineral.

[†] In particular, the Bourrée of the C major suite.

[‡] FractalMan, "Fractals in Nature," November 5, 2009, the Fractal Foundation, fractalfoundation.org.

[§] Michael Greenberg, "The Hallucinators Among Us," *New York Review of Books*, April 4, 2013.

We can easily extend the metaphor to say that human emotions and stories are fractal copies of emotions felt by other people in other times and places, like my mother's and my experience late in the fall in Maine. Could it be that what you are feeling and doing as the one and only you didn't start with you and won't end with you?

A man comes into a room, discovers his daughter on the telephone, and curses in German. He doesn't speak German at any other time, but his father used to explode when he found a member of the family on the telephone and his father spoke only German. In those days phone calls were expensive, but not anymore.

If we really examined the habits in our own lives, we would probably notice more and more recurring patterns, from the tilt of our heads, to a propensity to rearrange furniture, to the animals, or lack of them, we keep. We might notice that a person's intonation is a family trait, as is the way she walks, or the moods she displays. And then we might grow interested in larger patterns, such as general orderliness, or kinds of relationships or professional undertakings. One could argue that some are consciously adopted, and about some we have no clue; but one thing is undeniable: we are discovering that more and more of Nature is an evolving display that promises infinite variety in patterned form.

This might lead us to ask: When we act, who is it that is performing the deed? Considering the complex world of action and reaction around us, when a glass falls off the table after making contact with your elbow, or you forget to send out an important message, doesn't it make sense to be curious about how it all works, how the habits of our ancestors, and the different ages and parts of ourselves, and even a surge of radiation from a sunspot, may have come together at that critical moment?

Not the Doer

In general when we "take responsibility" for an action we are either doing so proudly or taking the blame. In either case, our attention is limited to personal concerns within a closed system, and we will miss all that is happening beyond its borders, such as another's viewpoint or emotional needs. Or we will become so preoccupied with remorse that we fail to do the obvious: get a dustpan and sweep up the glass, or make an instant course correction in relation to a message not sent. So while it is valid and sometimes quite useful to say that we are the actors in our lives, the doers of our actions, *insisting* that it is so places us squarely at that spot in the center of the universe we thought we had outgrown and closes the door on all the information (and grace) that lie beyond.

It takes a big person to resist the temptation to find fault with himself or with others. See what happens when, instead, you live into the story that you are not "the doer"; that you are embedded in evolving systems of infinite extension.

You may be wondering, does this mean I'm not responsible for any of my actions? Should we teach our children to do whatever they feel like and tell them they don't have to worry about the consequences? No, quite the contrary. Saying you are not the doer allows you to step into responsibility more fully than ever before. This is why: Under normal circumstances, when you make a "mistake" you start closing down, while casting around for someone or something to take the blame. If you blame someone else you have to build a story to support your accusation and make it airtight. If you blame yourself, you may close down even further in shame. In any case you retreat from the present world around you and become distracted from the goal at hand. The story that you are not the doer, on the other hand, prompts you to be curious and open and allows you to observe far more about the "mistake" than you did from the other frame. Then, going forward, you can smoothly make corrections. Think of how even the great tennis players, when they make an error, lose concentration, and will often get into a cycle where the loss of concentration induces another miss that guarantees a third. Any time you turn your attention to blaming yourself or others, you effectively drop out, abandoning the present moment where all the action takes place. I remember a time when my dog ran out in the street and was hit by a car. The conscientious driver got out of his car and stood by me while I was trying to comfort my injured dog and give a friend instruction as to how to get my car started. The hit-and-stay driver was so upset that he could only wring his hands and apologize loudly and profusely. Finally I had to fairly shout at the good man to go away, as he was doing nothing but obstructing me. Had he had access to the story that he was not the doer, he might have been able to relay my instructions to my friend and help me lift the dog into the car.

To support the "you are not the doer" story, consider this. Contrary to common sense, we don't even decide to act. Neurologists tell us that our brains register a decision a half second *after* we have made our move. We act first and decide later and are certain that it is the other way around. You are drawn into action by the story you are living into before your mind ever gets involved.

So let's tell ourselves that we can enhance the possibility of a particular outcome by doing our best, but we can't guarantee it because there are always other forces at work beyond our control. Imagine that you are rafting down a river. If you stay balanced and don't resist the current, you are likely to be able to get to the end of the journey, and with minimal use of the paddle. In one sense you could say, "I did it!" and celebrate your accomplishment, and that would be perfectly valid. And in another, for the pleasure of seeing partnerships in a wider frame, you could say, "I worked with the river, and together we arrived at the landing, and then the river went on." After all, isn't the whole universe at play wherever we are?

In the following story, the children of Remington Street all participated in an event where each was active and engaged, but none would be likely to be called the doer, in this tale of ecstasy.

CHAPTER TWENTY-TWO

Getting in Tune

UNTIL I WAS TEN, my family lived in Cambridge, Massachusetts, on Remington Street, a small crooked passageway connecting Massachusetts Avenue and Harvard Street. Because of a
bend in the road, cars were willy-nilly forced to slow down. Somehow we children of the neighborhood—the Stones, the Gafneys,
the Russos, and the Burkes—came to realize that this gave us the
advantage over the vehicles, and we claimed the street as our own.
We drew hopscotch grids on the tar and played double skip rope
from sidewalk to sidewalk. We often dropped our bikes hastily in
the middle of the street to join the next game. Over time, after two
in the afternoon, almost no automobiles chose that route.

Those were delicious days, days full of sensation. I remember
my happy heartbeat, the cold of the fall season on my face, and the
sounds of our voices, but the strongest body memory to which I

return often is the game of Double Dutch jump rope. Two children, standing on opposite sides of the street, turn a rope in each hand so that one rope makes an upward curve and one a downward curve in fast rotation. The trick for the players in the street is to get into the oscillating structure, jumping over each rope as it comes to the bottom and avoiding being hit by the other rope as it comes up. It's a rhythm thing. You listen for the slap of compressed air as each rope passes the ground and you watch the whizzing oscillations until you are breathing with it and then you run, jump in, stay for a few rounds, and whiz out again. Sometimes two kids run together into the center, and then it's amazing and you're laughing like crazy.

Incrementally the whole group of kids begins to get in sync with the action: the rhythm, heartbeat, breathing, running, jumping, and the whizzing in and out. The hands of the rope twirlers move with the jumpers at the correct speed and the kids breathe with one another, and when you get it right it's exhilarating. It's paradise.

Double Dutch is my image for the spin of the cosmos, from vibrant deep space, to the oscillations of the galaxies, down to the details of the dance of our days on earth. We can think of Nature as a process in flow, always in spin, always in motion, breathing in and breathing out, integrating the new into rising levels of coherence as she seeks an elusive equilibrium. The way I see it, you either get in tune with her or you don't, and if you don't, you're out.

TUNING IN DEEP

Colleen Quinn is a physical therapist living in the San Francisco area, with whom I had the good fortune to work after I had knee replacement surgery. At first I thought we weren't doing enough hard work and I became impatient. She would smile and give me an anatomy lesson, or tell me to ground my feet and fold over, my head, neck, and arms hanging free, and then have me use my core muscles (which were notably missing from my awareness) to bring me up to standing. She held me on track to wake up my muscles to their relationships with others throughout my body, and after a while I began to get comments such as "You look like you work out." I couldn't make sense of them at first because I didn't think Colleen and I were doing anything that would qualify. So then Colleen turned to waking up my brain to a new story of strength and mastery. Her narrative is a great example of tuning in to the cosmos, referencing patterns of many types, and so I share it for the most part in her direct words.

Colleen

When you are the ninth child of a family of ten, the number of things going on at any moment is mind-boggling. Out of a combination of intelligence and desperation, you somehow find a way of creating stability. I can remember being around eight years old at a big family meal, with the smell of gravy wafting in from the kitchen, and so many conversations sliding over one another and crashing into one another that I never knew what was happening.

What saved me from a descent into chaos was wallpaper. Our dining room wallpaper had a flower and leaf pattern that ran in textured rows up and down the height of the wall. The leaves coiled in circles, first one way and then the other, and the flowers were made from little spots of color. I loved how a series of tiny dots created a petal, and those petals, a flower. Each link I made between the tiniest elements on their way to forming a bigger picture provided a burst of inner satisfaction. This fertile field of wallpaper, with its parts to count and dots to organize, gave me safe harbor to which I could return throughout my childhood.

My interest in tracing patterns soon went beyond its primary function of providing a safe space for me and took on a life of its own. Kneeling in church as a child, surrounded by musky incensed air and the drone of hymns and gospel, I looked to the pattern of pillars and pews on either side of the aisle, and assessed them for symmetry. Calculating one grand cement pillar for every six pews, my mind would then expand to consider the construction process of the high-vaulted ceilings held by these supports before it came back to study the detailed adornment at the end of each wooden row.

My long-time fascination with pattern found satisfaction through high school and college in the study of art history, the geology of mountain ranges, and the arrangement of celestial bodies in the cosmos. So as I started out on my life's work as a physical therapist, my eyes were prepped to appreciate pattern everywhere. I remember the day in gross anatomy lab in my third year of college when we had to dissect out the trapezius muscle from its attachments at the head and shoulder of a cadaver. I had studied this muscle in isolation via flash cards, looked at it on a diagram, and memorized its action, origin, and insertion points. I repeated the word "trapezius" until I could roll it off my tongue, but it remained a thing in isolation until this defining moment.

I was able to see suddenly that there, beneath the skin, this muscle was also one simple dot in a glorious network of interconnected dots, making up a stunning pattern. I turned to the five other nervous physical therapy students to share this revelation, but they didn't look up. They were concentrating on the solitary body lying there on the cold steel dissection table, reeking of formaldehyde.

Despite its stillness, the body now appeared to me as a large dynamic pattern, made up of smaller and smaller related patterns: an inward pattern that seemed to me to echo so many other patterns I had studied, as far out as the stars. This "dot" of muscle was attached via tendons to the bones of the skull, spine, and shoulder. It was nourished with oxygen from the blood cells that are pumped from the heart and charged with impulses that travel from a point in the brain along the spinal cord, through nerve roots to its muscle belly. The trapezius muscle is completely useless on its own. But through the right connections, it can help lift your coffee cup to your lips or pull a loved one in close—all triggered by your simple desire to do so.

Sparked by the wonder of how such systems come alive, I stood over the corpse on the dissection table and tuned in to this richness I had just discovered. Buoyed on waves of fascination and curiosity, I set off to heal the world.

Over the last twenty years, the type of rehabilitation we do has evolved radically with further understanding of connections throughout the body as a whole. I now am clear that awareness of thoughts and feelings is as important as length and strength of muscles, and have come to appreciate deeply how they influence one another in a continuous feedback loop.

Our built-in reflexes were intended to help us survive; and so we have. But now they are being chronically triggered by normal worries or fears or the need for protection against the kinds of impulsive movements we make when we are distracted or stressed. Because the world most of us live in is increasingly complex, we hold tension in our bodies, our muscles overcompensate, and then we get into pain and things begin to break down. Often it is just this process that is a wake-up call to build a stronger mind-body connection that will make us better fit for the world today. My motto is, if we can get ourselves into these cycles, we can undo them, and initiate healthier ones.

Often when people come to see me, they want to strengthen isolated muscle groups so that they will look better. Or they want me to rid them, immediately, of a painful syndrome in a joint; and indeed most of the prescriptions I receive from doctors order just that. Others want me to push them to work up a sweat, in an obsessive attempt to dominate their reluctant bodies. But I have a totally different agenda. I greet each new client as an unexplored ecosystem that is doing its best to integrate each dot of tissue and bone into a patterned whole on the way to creating a flow between the inside and the random stimuli of the outer world.

The first thing I concentrate on is awareness: awareness of the breath and its ability to create spaciousness in the body. As muscles around the lungs expand, there is more room for bones and soft tissue to move freely. I point awareness toward the inside of the body to feel what it is like to move gracefully, muscles and bones gliding with intention and purpose, rather than grinding over each other just to get the job done. I put focus on grounding the feet and feeling the support of the legs to create stability in the core, allowing a funnel of energy to move up through the spine, rib cage, heart, and out through the top of the head, energy extending infinitely beyond our perceived physical body.

The result of making these relationships conscious is a sense of our bodies as something more than a thing we drag around to complete tasks. As we practice feeling these linkages, we start to perceive how the energy of our thoughts and perceptions directs and affects our bodies in a very real way. The more conscious we become of how these systems interrelate, the more we will be able to align with them by choosing behaviors that serve to help, heal, and support them, as well as guide them to do what we want them to do. In my experience, this is the gateway to discovering a powerful internal sense of self.

When all is integrated, the self is free to expand to include a universally connected consciousness.

Last week I was having a day that I kept trying to convince myself was just a bad hair day, in an attempt to lighten my mood. Toward evening I had an impulse that took no thought at all. I poured ice and white wine into a mason jar, called to the dogs, and drove down to the Pacific Ocean. I sat in the sand and watched the waves sliding over one another, breathing in and breathing out, flowing over and withdrawing from the rocks in a silky caress. I had a thought that I've often had around the ocean, which always feels like home to me: "You came from here." But this evening particularly, I felt every dot inside me connect to the sea, and I came away with firsthand knowledge that there is no separation, no separation anywhere.

—

Colleen has transformed the somewhat chaotic flavor of her child-hood into the sense of secure attachment in the arms of the whole universe. Her life is a wonderful example of a self-organizing emergent system. Her fascination with fractal patterns protected her from the intrinsic turmoil of a family of twelve and helped her to discover deeper layers of order in herself and in the extension of herself into the world. As she increased her knowledge, she was able to tune in to her body in a remarkable way and teach us to tune in to ours.

In several of the stories in this book, we see how important the integration of mind and body is to growth, achievement, and well-being. Think of how the beliefs surrounding her blindness restricted Jessica's movements, such that her head remained still and her hands hung by her side as though "encased in stone," so she was unable to fully express herself in her singing. Or how the children in Puebla came together over "Twinkle, Twinkle, Little Star" when Ben got them out of their seats to move in rhythm and smile. The upgrading of a story from child to adult helps bring about that integration, such that we often see a sudden ease of movement in the world, an "in-tune-ness," after a transformation of this kind. Look how John, who saved the cliffs from unwanted development, was able to move from a resistant posture smoothly into connection once he had cast the townspeople in a new story, and how the tension immediately left my body when I said, "Everything I do at the cabin is writing," which allowed me to write chapters, go for walks, take naps, wash dishes, and dream.

CHAPTER TWENTY-THREE

Extreme Participation

I WAS WRITING ABOUT JUST this sort of thing when I left the cabin one morning to get a break. Outdoors, I looked up to find the day was exceptionally brilliant, even for June. Then I had an experience of being so in tune with nature that I lost any sense of identity or agency. It started with my noticing that the air seemed to quiver and pulse with excitement. I was prompted to sing—why not? No one was around to judge me. I bounced along singing with enthusiasm, slowing down here and there to embrace in spirit the birds and branches that seemed in spirit to be embracing me.

And then a great horned owl glided in silence up from the underbrush on my left and crossed over into the darker woods. I was awestruck. *How very peculiar,* I thought. *It's noon! Owls aren't supposed to be awake at noon.* The owl had sailed by only a few feet from me in its soundless passage into the forest. Then a hundred yards or so ahead two hawks flew up in tandem from the bushes to my left, and again flew quite directly in front of me. I felt thoroughly blessed and highly curious, while my mind was struggling to give a rational explanation for what I sensed was an out-of-the-ordinary happening. Perhaps I should go on with my exuberant singing? I continued as the little birds of the cranberry bog appeared to me to be chattering ever closer. The water was certainly flashing unusually brightly, and the plants along the edge of the bog positively radiated green.

Sometime later I came to the top of a knoll that looks down on a crooked path, and heard a *whoosh* above my head. An owl, I fancy *the* owl, flew over me, landed on a branch at my eye level, and faced me. My mind raced around the impossible idea of trying to get a photograph, but then quieted down. We looked at each other for a long time. I thought, *We're exchanging information, that's what we're doing,* and then without a sound she sailed deep into the woods.

Farther on, I came up close to a small tree on the side of the path and for no known reason found myself musing about the concept of loneliness. Watching an ant crawling up the trunk, I had the thought, or more likely the feeling, *Impossible to be lonely, ever, since we have each other.* And I was startled in the next moment to realize that what I meant by "we" was the combination of Roz, tree trunk, and ant on the crawl. Really. Here we were, we band of three become one; or better, one become three. All equal.

I was not my ordinary self. I was a being in some kind of polygamous relationship with an ant and a sapling. In other words, I was out of my mind.

I had left my mind behind and slipped into a state of extreme participation with the world around me—similar, perhaps, to what Colleen experienced watching the waves of the Pacific. You could call it being alive, but not life as we ordinarily experience it. I was as vibrant as is everything else, my cells oscillating on some universal wavelength.

I told a friend, a physicist, about the experience, and he explained that there are three levels upon which we can connect. "Being present" with clarity and joy is the first. The second he referred to as a "cellular level" where the boundaries of time and space are blurred and you are likely to be attuned to what is going to happen next. In my childhood I heard often the story that my grandmother, traveling by train between New York and Hartford, had alerted the passengers in her railway car to an upcoming train wreck well before there were any signs of impending trouble. This is not unusual—many families, it seems, carry such stories of attunement on the cellular level.

My experience in the trio with ant and sapling seemed to fit my friend's description of the third, deepest level. At this level your atoms and your consciousness are in resonance with all other atoms. Strange things happen here. Trees reach out to touch you. Birds draw you in. You are in ecstasy and you are in love.

Anomalous Experience: Out in the Open

After that experience in the bog, I was bursting to tell people about it, but whenever I came close to the subject I stopped short. Who would be interested? Who would not think me some refugee from the New Age? So I told only the few people I thought would be on the same wavelength, and in order to create connection, I decided to ask other people idle questions about anomalous experiences they might have had.

One of the times I had a chance to do so was on a visit to a winery in Paso Robles, California. I was seated at dinner next to the ranch's original farmer, Mitch, who is now retired. He had come back to the vineyard to take visitors like me on a tour of what looked like miles of rows of carefully tended grapevines undulating over hills, interspersed with the occasional coastal oak, each one a tree of considerable age and magnitude. Perhaps because all of this was so new to me, I found myself asking him if he had ever had an experience that had changed him significantly.

Mitch told me he'd spent the first part of his working life raising vegetables, and in his forties he took a job in this vineyard, which was at that time a new venture, for both Mitch and the vines. Farming of any kind is difficult work, but this was particularly trying for Mitch because he didn't have a feel for grapes, which meant he had to make decisions piecemeal, decisions such as on which hillside to plant a particular variety, when and what to prune on a hundred acres of grapevines, or how much water to give the plants, if any at all. But none of it made any real sense to him. It was like the listener's experience wandering aimlessly around a piece of music he has never heard before. Then one day, he told me, he was in the vineyard in one of the "blocks" of rows, and as he stood there in the sunshine, pinching off a dead bit on one of the plants, this vineyard—which had seemed so foreign—flowed into him, right through his feet. It bathed his whole body, it entered his cells, it suffused his brain, and it was there to stay. "That was it," Mitch said, "it never left." He remembers the exact instant of his transformation. He remembers which of the thousands of plants he was idly pruning. From then on, every decision flowed naturally, every part of the farming of grapes made intuitive sense. There was no longer any separation between Mitch and the vines.

It didn't sound to me as though Mitch had simply hung around long enough to learn about grapes, partly because he reported that the change happened all at once. I warrant that Mitch had what Barbara McClintock, who won the Nobel Prize for her discovery of "jumping genes" in relation to corn, called "a feeling for the organism."

When I first met Mitch, out in the vineyard, he was slightly distracted because he was concerned about delivering an injured owl to an agency that could oversee its recovery. He struck me as an unusual soul, deeply connected to the earth and her creatures.

If you ask people if they have had any transformational moments in their lives or any truly unusual experiences, many say no somewhat dismissively, but more people than you might guess say yes and are happy to tell you about the voice he heard in his head in a momentous, emotional moment, or the moose that appeared in the driveway as her mother lay dying. They may tell you how the day started with the traffic lights turning green all the way to work, and how every conversation all day long moved a certain project forward. So I choose to think that these alchemical occurrences are not widely talked about simply because they are not mainstream thinking and might bring about a derisive response.

Let's pick up this conversation. Ask other people, even your close friends, whether they have undergone an out-of-the-ordinary or unique occurrence that changed them, and give them a chance to articulate and bring to life whatever lies dormant for them in the arena of what we refer to as anomalous experience. These are the stories of restoration and attunement that qualify us as partners in evolution. Start the conversation; see where it goes. After all, we may find out down the road that the phenomena that we now call magic only appear to be mystical in light of our current understanding of the laws of nature. Maybe others, birds included, actually *can* sense the magnetic field of your heart. When you are feeling happy, expansive, and free, watch to see if they take steps to move (or hop) a little closer.

On Consciousness

Now let's leap to a wider frame. Let's pretend that the cosmos is a giant web where every point is connected to every other point, and every point holds the information of the entire universe in the palm of its metaphorical hand. Or in a more dynamic image, perhaps we could conjure the concept of the universe as a giant termite mound, where each individual, by action and reaction, knows what part to play to grow and maintain the whole. Here we stumble over the question of consciousness. Are termites conscious? Probably not in the sense of self-consciousness, but in the loop of taking in data, reacting, and putting new data out? Absolutely. Consciousness in this definition is a feedback loop: data received, altered, and sent back out again. So nothing ever stays the same; action builds on reaction, and the system evolves.

And how do you or I fit into this universe? If you are not the doer, who are you? Perhaps we might spin the story that we are conduits through which the underlying nature of the universe reveals itself. You might say in your own words, "I make it manifest," and you would mean "make the cosmos manifest the way a warm greeting brings to the surface the underlying relationship I have with a friend, or the way a singer reveals the life and the truth in the music." And then you might have to be patient, and still, and watch for a response: data sent out, received, and sent back again in altered form.

The "I" in "I make it manifest" is not ego; it is a device, like "I am not the doer," that you half invent, half discover, and that opens a new category of experience. Our normal way of viewing things is by agency or its close cousin, cause and effect: when something happens we look to see how it came about in a linear view of the way things work. We trace the breaking of a glass back to the elbow that knocked it off the table, and perhaps to the loud noise that startled the person attached to that elbow: A affects B, B affects C, et cetera. At the next level, we name the field of the story, the one we are living into, as the culprit, the source of the accident. If you were to say, "Of course I would break that glass! I have ADHD (story) and I am so very clumsy (more story)," unbeknownst to you, you would be increasing the likelihood of another mishap. If you were privy to the phenomenon of fields, you might say, "My stories are heading me into more accidents." And you would start to loosen their effect.

Stories truly are fields. They deal in probabilities or odds; they don't operate in the certainty of cause and effect. They accomplish what they do by energetic interactions across space and time, like my mother's melancholy popping up in my heart. The story we call possibility, in particular, creates a radiant, loving field of energy that facilitates an alignment between people and their circumstances.

This new tier offers an additional distinction to play with: I invent and accept that I am a channel for information. I behave in harmony with the rest of the universe, as an evolver, and it is my privilege to move in partnership with the flow of evolution. Information comes into me and is altered and processed by my cells. I send it out again, changed. It gets processed and altered by the cells of others and comes back to me in a feedback loop that, with hitches here and there, continues to higher degrees of complexity and integration. This new story I am walking in makes me conscious of how at each moment either I am a partner with the cosmos in its ongoing effort to rebalance itself, like Peg Howard in her inspirational connection with the Japanese businessmen, and Sam the toddler flower picker when he upgraded his story, or I am carelessly obstructing its process. Think this: every time a story changes from child form to adult, a blockage to the universe's movement to find equilibrium is dissolved across space and time. The Third Reich was a child story based on hierarchy, absolute obedience, and the need for approval, one in which only one kind of human being was deemed important. Apartheid in South Africa was one of myriad other stories based in child thinking. The transformation of a child story, of which the Truth and Reconciliation Commission in South Africa is an example, initiates a new resonance pattern and new feedback loops. On every scale.

Our great human gift, comparable to the ant's communication and rebuilding skills, is the ability to tell one another our stories of healing and renewal. We reconcile by acts, and words; we restore through how we relate and how we grow; we inspire through what we build and the art we make; and we cure ourselves by how we care for others and what we give away. In those ways we bring our hearts into a collective resonance.

And that is where the power lies. Addressing the dizzying feats of communication, farming, and construction that termites accomplish, management consultant Meg Wheatley reminds us that no matter how patient we are, no matter how observant, we will never see one termite alone build a single tower. Because it is integral to our new story of the cosmos as a giant web where every point is connected to every other, it follows that everything we do and say affects all else. There is no escape: what we say, and how we say it, counts.

Faced with the bewildering complexity of our new role, let's take some baby steps in expanding our minds to balance some contradictions we've introduced on this journey. According to Barry Lopez, author of *Arctic Dreams*, we are in a sense compelled to do so: "If there is a stage at which an individual life becomes truly adult, it must be when one grasps the irony in its unfolding and accepts responsibility for a life lived in the middle of . . . paradox."

Now we can call on our brains to help us because they have a mechanism, a switch that can take us from one concentration to another in rapid succession. I ask you, can you hold the "real world" before you—your family at dinner, or the article you just read, or your current worry, or that new baby, and (switch) perceive that everything is story? Can you imagine and hold in mind, for instance, that you might be wrong about what you firmly believe regarding such things as talent, or messages in crop circles, or germ theory? Can you feel something acutely in the present, like anger or disappointment or guilt, and (switch) almost simultaneously feel it as a memory of another time? Are you able to perceive yourself in one context as someone who accomplished a project and then (switch) see yourself in another context as not the doer, but the expression of a larger fractal pattern? Are you able to go about life in a practical manner, turning doorknobs to open doors, making five-year plans, and playing rock, paper, and scissors, and at the same time appreciate that solidity is an illusion and that whatever you envision five years from now will almost certainly not be there when you get there because you-and-the-world will have changed? Are you able to put front and center the contradiction that people are patterned to seek material growth—clearly the source of wealth—and material growth is impoverishing? Can you find the music in all this and sense where it wants to go?

CHAPTER TWENTY-FOUR

Global Partners

THROUGHOUT THE CHAPTERS OF this book we have been developing an ever-expanding definition of maturity in order to take a step farther into the territory of being adult. First we rewrote childish narratives to reflect a more grown-up perspective, and then followed practices that strengthened us to look for new and different truths, and then moved to attune ourselves with broader systems, which involved mirroring nature's processes. Now with our newfound adult capacity to embrace ambiguity and to contemplate the way things are without the need to be right or to avoid what we don't want to see, let's look at the story of who we have been on the planet and discover in more depth what we might become.

From the time we settled down on "farms," about twelve thousand years ago, we humans have been busily using our formidable brains to competitive advantage, and we have made staggering gains. Causing extinction in other species is not new—we've been doing that for millennia—but over the last two centuries our explosive progress that has us reaching into all corners of the globe qualifies us as an honest-to-goodness Invasive Species. And lest we feel diminished by that appellation, we can always add that we take the prize as the *most* invasive species on earth, just by doing what species are designed to do to optimize survival: establish territory, seek to possess, and dominate.

An invasive species is one that disrupts the stability of the ecosystem it enters by interfering with controls that maintain variety and balance. I think of a book my granddaughter loves, with a picture of a sea otter on the cover. The otter is lying playfully on its back, cradling a sea urchin on its belly. Sea otters, sea urchins, and kelp, I found out, form a more or less balanced system. The urchins eat the kelp, the otters eat the sea urchins, and a kelp forest gives the sea otters a place to hide from ravenous sharks. If another species captures the sea otters for their fur, or they are driven away, the sea urchins multiply and eat themselves out of house and home. Now there is no food left for the urchins, and no hiding place for the otters should the few be inclined to return. Write this large and we get an inkling of the enormous, vital interdependent system that is our earth, where things are perpetually shifting and evolving in one dazzling rebalancing act.

Truth be told, we no longer live in the wild, and haven't for generations, even if we regularly hike in parks, or go camping in the summer, or live on the edge of conservation land. We inhabit an environment that is entirely reflective of ourselves, except perhaps in the very extreme conditions at the outer edges of the earth—but even in those desolate places we can entertain the idea that we could be reached by helicopter if necessary. Not for the last fifteen thousand years have we been prompted to settle in shadows near the edges of the forest to avoid big cats roaming the plains. We have no predators, except of our own kind. Go from window to window in your house. Can you see any view that doesn't have the stamp of human dominance on it? Look carefully.

So we are likely to be increasingly out of touch with how nature works, making it difficult to reap the benefits of aligning with her systemic ways. Given how things have evolved, we would be prone to think that our minds and nature operate independently of each other. As Gregory Bateson, that brilliant student of learning and evolution, noted, it's all one: "You can't lop off any loops in the system." We think we can decide that Lake Erie will be a good place to toss some of the garbage of human life, but we forget that the eco-mental system called Lake Erie is a part of our wider eco-mental system. In other words, in his oft-quoted statement, if Lake Erie is driven insane, so are we.

We have seen how the unexamined patterns of our earliest forms of attachment, secure or ambivalent, disorganized or distant, may affect us throughout our lives. We may be either strengthened through those early bonds or left vulnerable to relational difficulties, or both. Now let's widen that frame. In a similar manner, could it be that how we are connected to all of nature and her processes—the vigor of our affiliation—has the power to make us ill or well?

On a basic level, it appears that simply being in a setting with plants and trees makes us smarter at least. Marc Berman at the University of Michigan set out to see if he could actually measure a difference. He gathered thirty-eight students, gave them cognitive testing, and sent them out to take a three-mile walk. Half of them strolled along a busy street, the other half in a nearby arboretum. They were tested again on their return. The nature walkers showed dramatic cognitive gains over those who were subjected to people and traffic.* Other research reveals that seeing videos of the most gorgeous landscapes has no more positive effect on our brains than

---

* Daniel B. Smith, "Is There an Ecological Unconscious?," *The New York Times Magazine*, January 27, 2010.

staring at a blank wall, while looking out the window at hills and sky reads to our hungry minds as necessary nourishment.

The major problems in the world, said Dr. Bateson, are the result of the difference in the way nature works and the way people think. Well, I would add, only perhaps in the sense that nature embraces all species and their ways of contributing and surviving, and we humans have just been looking after ourselves. That would have been okay, had we not been so clever, and unknowingly engineered a change in management, a shift in our relationship to nature. The earth that used to be in charge is now to a great degree working through us, and we are still for the most part looking out for our own advantage. So the good news is that we are already partners in her evolution, and the challenge is that if we are going to make this system work we will have to step into her shoes as well as our own.

From her shoes we would probably see more and differently without the practical imperative. We might be tempted to learn about the delicate interdependencies in ecological systems that we currently break unwittingly. Here's one I just became aware of because I had some dead branches removed from the trees around the cabin and realized I didn't hear anymore the friendly little woodpecker I enjoyed in the mornings. So I did some research and found out that when we cut down dead trees, we remove the woodpeckers' housing and food supplies, compelling them to leave the area. Without woodpeckers, bark beetles multiply freely and kill the trees, spreading the pine pitch canker that kills many more trees. If we act as nature's partners, those systems would come under our freshly watchful eyes, just as we might notice how the way our traffic lights are set hinder or facilitate people getting to work.

It could be that being out of touch with nature's processes is related to the carelessness with which we sever connections, even among ourselves, through divorce or simple ignorance of children's needs, not to mention all-out tribal warfare. We know now that the early patterns of attachment we absorbed have an impact; where the attachment was not sufficiently secure, the growth and transformation that is the natural pattern gets blocked, slows down, and we get out of sync with others. Let's assume that the quality of our attachment to "mother nature" has a similar effect. If we can't get a constant and robust feel for the natural systems close to us, how can we expect to respond meaningfully to droughts across the globe or to the melting of the ice sheets?

There is a lot of bad-mouthing of the human race going on these days, what with pollution and the poisoning of the atmosphere, populations in abject poverty, and ethnic wars popping up like wildflowers. But let's give ourselves a break. We are only living out our survival patterns on a large scale, just as Alan was doing on a smaller fractal scale until the big betrayal that caused him to pause and reflect. He had no idea what a mess he was making of his relationships until then, and his mind was no help to him. So let's look on ourselves in a dispassionate way and realize that we have had no clue that what was required of us was to create a new story, and an adult one at that, which would take us beyond the survival patterns that have had us looking to exploit everything in our path. It seems not to have occurred to us that incessant material growth might be just the wrong thing for us. So let's walk outdoors, and walk some more. We can absorb natural processes simply by moving in their midst: like a parent's love, they just rub off on us. Then we can think about the new story we want to create that will ease our suffering and that of the world we inhabit.

THE NEXT STORY

First it would be wise to remind ourselves of the child story we are embedded in, and the safety pattern we have been governed by throughout our lives. Like all child stories, it features the hero, mankind, at the center of the narrative. The Eighth Psalm of the Bible offers us a fair synopsis: God has made man to have dominion over all of His works, and all of nature lies under man's feet. Nature is to be conquered, tamed, and stepped on, apparently, and is there for man's purposes. I loved this psalm as a child and memorized it. The sound of the language was delicious to me. Listen to this, for example: "When I consider thy heavens, the work of thy fingers, the moon and the stars, which thou hast ordained . . ." or this: "thou hast put all things under his feet: All sheep and oxen, yea, and the beasts of the field; the fowl of the air, and the fish of the sea, and whatsoever passeth through the paths of the seas." It is an exemplary child story, and I used to recite its pleasant rhythms and affirming sentiments to myself before I went to sleep. But it is time for an upgrade.

Remember, all survival strategies contain the shadow of a cataclysmic moment, the ghost of the past threatening to return, because safety patterns are not geared to the present, but relate instead to the entirely different conditions of the time when the pattern was conceived. The control that this pattern promised is eroding before our eyes, which, depending on how deeply we feel it, makes us ripe for change.

In building the new story let's look to our definitions. Let's reiterate that nature is not a thing but an emerging, self-organizing system, a *process* of continuous evolution toward more and more complex, diverse, beautiful, and mutually enhancing relationships. As her partner, we are in an evolving process, too, within and without, opening to new information, letting go of resistance, looking for beauty we haven't seen before, searching and listening for evolving order.

When we act without awareness in a child's story, we are likely to forge ahead, taking what we need in the assumption that some adult figure will handle the rest. But when we are centered in the adult in us, the part that has grown past the stories of the child, we lean on our vibrant connection to all of consciousness, not some higher power that we imagine is there in order to give us what we want. It is our privilege to attune ourselves to the artistry of nature, comingling with but not overriding her creativity, bringing a unique perspective from each one of us to add to the evolution happening through and around us. This adult story may even promise a solution to the condition that, disconnected as we are, we are pretty much all starved for love.

Setting the Stage for Questions

It isn't usual that people consult the universe for guidance, but it is an excellent practice. I play a game where I imagine a wise being, Altair, named for one of the stars of the Northern Hemisphere's Summer Triangle, who lives in a forest of my imagination. When I have a question where the answer is not obvious to me, I go through a process in my mind in which I search for Altair. Invariably I find him in an elevated place among the trees that takes a bit of effort to get to. I greet him politely and respectfully and I ask him my question. Then I relax my mind and wait. He answers sooner or later, and sometimes his response surprises me. At any rate it is never what I would expect, or I would have thought of it myself.

What if we were to give ourselves a mantra in the form of a question to keep in mind: "Is this plan of action in tune, or is it off-track?" Science has recently uncovered so many secrets heretofore undreamed of that our mantra plunges us into ambiguity and nuance. It invites us to look two ways: first, inside ourselves to see whether what we are contemplating will expand us and help us to grow, or whether it is, perhaps, a repetition of a survival pattern hidden under a veneer of sophistication.

In this regard, let me tell you about a client with whom I worked who was very adventuresome. A reporter at large, he took assignments in some of the most dangerous war zones in the world. He would perhaps argue that these experiences stretched him and helped him to grow and in some ways he would be right; but on reflection he could also tell you that courting danger was his survival pattern. As a child he had been badly mistreated and at the same time kept under lock and key, so his impulse was always to get away from home, while at the same time he longed for love from the people who were abusing him. The dangers he embarked on as an adult allowed him to feel like his own person. Women were attracted to this brave and apparently carefree soul, so the prospect of finding love was a promise ever at hand—and because he was always on the move he avoided the stage in any relationship when he would feel the necessity and the fear of giving up some freedom. This survival pattern produced excitement and riches of many kinds, but as discussed in chapter 7, it brought him no closer to enjoying secure attachment than what he experienced as a child. It therefore kept alive both his search and his longing.

Second, the question "Is this plan of action in tune, or is it off-track?" asks us to look outside ourselves; to expand our range of inquiry as to whether, in the larger scheme of things, the project we are undertaking or the item we are buying has supported or exploited people or resources along the way. The world can no longer return to a wild state while we are on board, so our questions had best consider the partnership and aim toward getting us better connected. "What would be a more compassionate or generative way of doing things?" we might ask. "Through the practice of what art may I expand my heart?" (Make sure you wait for your Altair's reply.) We will probably never be able to answer these questions with complete certainty, but simply asking them and listening for a response qualifies us as companions in evolution.

COEVOLVERS

You can see that a transducer has only to clear the channel of his being, and to be a coevolver doesn't mean that you have to do big things. If you cradle a baby with love and provide consistency you are attuned to nature's magnificent processes. You could even be starting a new fractal pattern, or consciously continuing an old one, and who knows what a gift that will make to your infant, and to generations going forward? If you write a letter to a newspaper and intend to contribute to a reader's awareness, or run a hardware store that increases the spirit of community by its welcoming environment, you are doing just what I am talking about. If you are a restaurant chain and you are reducing your prices to undercut local eating places, you are probably behaving just like Andean pampas grass, or the cane toad, reducing diversity and discouraging local participation. Or if you are so big that you are isolated from criticism, and no "predator" wants to challenge you, or you feel so successful that you ignore signs of moving times, we would say you are off-track for nature's purposes. An invasive species is part of nature, too, but it is an error that propagates itself, and like the sea urchin with no otters to stop it, it will eventually eat itself out of house and home. Then it's out.

A Common Problem with a Natural Solution

I receive letters, now and again, asking for my advice on personal matters. In my mind, however, there is nothing "personal," and those issues that are so labeled tend to be more aptly thought of as deeply human. A solution to "personal" problems is often best found by widening the frame and looking at who we are as a species, then following the dictates of Nature.

Here is a letter that arrived in the mail recently.

Dear Roz,

I have a problem with my teen daughter. I'm treasurer at a food cooperative, and last year, she stole all our savings money, totaling nearly $2,000. The cooperative has demanded that she pay back what she stole, but my daughter told me she has spent all the money. I have told her she needs to get a job, but she refuses, and there's no way I can force her. She's turned sixteen and she's not motivated at all to study or to work. The cooperative, for which I have spent years of my life working as a volunteer, has put me under pressure to either give back the money, or they will contact the police. I really don't know what to do.

A Desperate Father

If you, the reader, are like most of us, you will have an opinion about the two characters and what should be done. You might be more liberal than some, or more conservative. You might waver between treating the situation as one demanding punishment or psychological assessment. It's a state of affairs that has torn many a family apart.

When I read it, my mind went in a different direction—to Monty Roberts, the original horse whisperer. At the very same time that Dr. Spock's *Baby and Child Care* was published, Monty Roberts was beginning to formulate his ideas on training wild horses that evolved to be as transformational for domestic human/animal relationships as Dr. Spock's were for parents and children of our own species. Raised in Nevada on rodeo grounds, Monty Roberts was privy as a child to all the thrills, violence, and cruelty in the relationship between men and horses that happens so often when men are exploiting animals for competition and profit. His father was a traditional horse "breaker," a man who was convinced that mustangs would respond to nothing short of fear. The job of the trainer, in brief, was to terrify each young horse into submission and to inflict pain to such a degree that its will was broken. Arising out of this combination of excitement and trauma, Monty forged a different path, using nature as a partner and his understanding of nature's ways as his guide.

The young Monty's familiarity with horses, coupled with an entrepreneurial leaning, got him a job at the age of thirteen with the rodeo, working on a team to round up mustangs and bring them in from the plains. Exposed to much that was new to him, Monty saw many of his inherited assumptions about horses overturned. He started to have opinions of his own about what the team should and shouldn't do; he felt strongly that they shouldn't break up families, or bring in lactating mares and leave the colts to die. So in his fourteenth summer, and for three summers thereafter, the young Monty crossed the Sierra Nevada to the high desert and lived in the company of mustangs, camping out under the stars, devoid of human company, to better understand the wild horses' ways.

Coming from a culture raging with testosterone, Monty was surprised to discover that it was the female, not the male, that was always the leader of the band. When youngsters would become unruly, the dominant female would push them to the outer edge of the group as punishment and hold them there with her gaze until she decided to allow them to return. She relied on their need for the herd to keep them in line. Monty had known that the mustang's counterreflex was to flee when frightened, but what he learned was that the herding instinct was stronger still. He observed carefully the mustangs' ways of communicating, which they did mostly in silence. He saw that they used body postures to send messages and employed gestures and facial expressions to signal such meanings as obedience or a desire to join, or as a command to the other to stay away. He saw all this as a language that he called "Equus."

Out of these experiences with herds of mustangs in the western high desert, Monty Roberts developed his signature horse training method; it is one that generates no fear, and applies no pain or undue force. With his process, in less than half an hour he can reliably "join up" with a wild horse that has never before been in contact with a human being. It is something that will give you goose bumps to watch, and very likely have you in tears.

I wrote back to Desperate Father, sending him a shortened version of the following description of Monty's method, because of its relevance to his daughter and, indeed, to most of humanity. It goes like this: Monty leads a frightened filly into a round pen about fifty feet in diameter. Because she is afraid, he encourages her to run away—to run the fear out of her system. She runs as far away from him as she can, which, of course, is around the perimeter of the pen. There are only two directions available to her and he encourages her to try both for as long as she feels the need. Eventually she slows down, her fear exhausted, with a parallel rise in her desire to join with a herd. The only living creature available to her is the man calmly standing in the center. She signals in "Equus" that she is ready to come in by cocking an ear toward him, by licking and chewing with her mouth, and by lowering her head to the ground. Through these gestures, Monty has discovered, the wild horse is communicating that she eats grasses, not meat, and therefore won't harm him, and is ready to take him on as her master or matriarch. At this moment, to reduce any sense of confrontation, Monty turns his body sideways to her and casts his eyes away. With that, she moves toward him, and when she touches him with her muzzle, Monty, still with his side toward her, reaches out and strokes her forehead. This is what he calls "Join Up," and this is the sequence that every wild horse Monty has trained follows, and there have been thousands. It is the portion of his work that I thought of after reading the letter from the desperate father.

Here is the rest of my letter to "Desperate Father":

I have often used the image of the round pen in situations like yours. A human being, like the horse, is also a herd animal, which is why Monty's work is relevant to your story, and incidentally why solitary confinement is so agonizing for prisoners. But while the horse is wired to flee, a person is designed to fight. So you have to allow room for your daughter to fight—she won't need much encouragement—but you want her to fight within a context. If the horse had been able to flee in any direction, it would obviously have been the end of her connection to Monty. Fighting will only be useful to your daughter, and to the relationship between the two of you, if you can design the equivalent of a "round pen." I don't of course mean one made out of stone and mortar, but something equally containing that affords her the chance to both fight and join up. And, miracle of miracles, you have the perfect setup for it! You can arrange things so that the combination of the police and the Food Co-op work as the walls of the pen, leaving you to be the trainer in the middle who can provide the comfort of the herd, once your daughter has had enough fighting.

So here is my suggestion. Tell her she has to make an arrangement to pay back the money and commit to getting a job, and tell her you will help her figure it out. If she says NO, which we assume she will, you tell her that the food cooperative is planning to report her to the police, but is willing to hold off for forty-eight hours (it could be longer but not much). Why? Because you asked them to. Only if she really believes you will you have a secure round pen. So be calm, and don't add any drama from your side, and be firm and solid as a rock. Let her shout that she hates you, that you don't love her and never have, let her attribute every kind of meanness to you, let her say "I don't care" (test), and let her walk away. If you truly understand the benefit to a human being of being allowed to express its nature when frightened, you will welcome the anger, and of course you will refrain from interpreting it or doing anything that could stoke the fire. Remember, Monty allowed his wild mustang to do what mustangs do when they are scared—flee—and you are allowing your daughter to do what humans do—fight. It means you are on track!

If you get frightened (or angry) in the process you will be tempted to fight back, but by all means resist the urge. If you don't, you will have slipped into the role of Monty's father and will end up just as desperate and helpless as you now feel. So tell her calmly you are available to talk and are willing to help her figure out how to move forward, but, you tell her, on the stroke of the hour two days hence (or whatever you decide is the right interval) you are going to release the Co-op, and if she has not come to an agreement with them, they will most likely have her arrested.

If she believes you, the problem will be over very soon. Don't worry, after a while she will love you more than ever. If she doesn't believe you, plug the holes in the side of the pen, and by that I mean make sure there is no one else she can run to who isn't enrolled in the plan, and would be likely to give her an exit. If she needs a little more fight time, and ends up

being arrested, think of it as simply another step in the
training. If you maintain a confident stance, she'll come
around eventually. It's her nature to do so.

Roz

Monty's work is extraordinary in that it frees all involved to be the true self, the infinite self behind the walking story, the one who is wired for love. It ends the destructive argument over whether the person acting out has the will to change. It's about following nature's dictates, cooperating with rather than opposing the way things are. It's a grown-up structure where things are not personal, and it's a way that has love and care radiating from the center. I have done versions of this intervention with a number of frightened people who are walking stories of anger: substance abusers, and anorexic teenagers, and young people who are out of control in other ways. As you can see, if you are able to create a solid round pen—and of course that is the key—everything that starts out as "personal" drains away. As the leader you are left in a position to be relaxed and loving, and as the person being helped you get to fight tooth and nail, express every bit of anger, and then you get to come home.

Desperate Father's letter is a single slice, a glimpse into a system that is seeking to balance itself and integrate new material—in other words, like all of nature, it is an emerging system seeking equilibrium at increasing levels of complexity. Isn't that also a description of "family"? By widening the frame and allowing us to see our own patterns in comparison and in contrast with those of another species, Monty Roberts has opened new pathways for our partnership with Nature.

CHAPTER TWENTY-FIVE

Renewal

THE STORIES YOU ARE about to read are about people who engage with life rapturously, and whose every move is designed to restore the spirit and promote its abundance. Like Monty, they have spent time deepening their understanding of their subjects in order to be able to exercise that quintessentially human gift for telling stories that heal and explanations that foster connections. And when it is time to take action, they do, in spades.

Nalini Nadkarni describes herself as a small brown woman scientist working in a little college in the Northwest, far away from money and power, by which she means New York and Harvard. Indeed, it is not her status or her appearance that commands authority. It's her passion for her work that would knock you over. She is a tree canopy expert, the natural extension of her tree-climbing habits as a young girl, she will tell you, and she has fallen in love with the verdant world at the top. When you get there, she says, you move through the clouds into what looks like an open field. There are plants up there that have adapted to draw nourishment from the mist, and creatures with special claws, like the sloth, for hanging out and down, and animals that never ever descend. Nalini is almost wild with desire to share with people how nature works. She wants you to experience the beauty, the biodiversity, and the complexity of the systems on the roof of the world. Apart from her research and data collecting, she reaches out by inviting different professions to explore the canopy together from different perspectives. She brought to the forest the dance troupe Capacitor, whose dancers modeled the process of growth as expressed through the human body. She convened visual artists among the trees so they might offer unique points of view on the shapes and ways of nature.

Nalini feels deeply sorry for people who have limited access to the outdoors. "How can I reconnect people with trees?" is her fervent cry. How can I get them to see and feel what I do when I am in the canopy? As a solution, she designed a project for prison inmates to grow mosses for the horticulture trade, thereby relieving the pressure on species of wild mosses that were being harvested for hanging baskets and flower arrangements. Equal beneficiaries were her captive students, who developed a reverence for nature, as well as a newfound pleasure in having something to offer. The program is spreading into more prisons, growing as it goes. Recently, inmates have been breeding frogs from a species that is close to extinction, raising them from tadpoles to adults until, to the prisoners' deep pleasure, they can be released into the wild, even as their caretakers remain behind.

Wondering how to engage more children to be interested and aware, Nalini bought up old Barbie dolls from a Goodwill center and had her team fit them out with hard hats and tree climbing gear. She sent them out with canopy manuals tucked under their arms to convince girls that women, as well as guys, can be scientists and researchers, and of course to introduce them to her beloved forest canopy. TreeTop Barbie, she's called, and she's a knockout.

"When we come to understand nature, we are touching the deepest part of ourselves," Nalini says. She felt impelled to share that knowledge of the interrelationships and the resplendent complexity and began to open people's eyes to fractal iterations in biology, dance, and art of the forms she saw in the trees. Just let her show you what she discovered about the pattern of blood vessels in our hearts—trees growing everywhere!

As Nalini understood, artists tend to be society's most gifted disrupters of the pragmatic outlook we adopted in our zeal to survive, and great artists produce many ways to help us experience those vital connections that take us beyond ourselves. Think of the *Pietàs* of Michelangelo, in which are embedded the spin and torque of nature carved into the marble, as well as the downward curves of grief and gentle arcs of love. Think of the all-over pattern of brushstrokes in a Monet or a Seurat that bring us into contact with the vibrations of the ether. Great music, especially because it exists in community, has the capacity to open us to the wide range of emotion and thought that is a gateway to entering the field of evolutionary partnership.

SING LESS, DREAM MORE

There is a song by Schubert called "The Dream of Spring" (*Frühlingstraum*) that transports us directly into the center of a universal paradox, stretching our minds and spinning our hearts. It shows us the way nature operates to integrate life's multiple strands, and calls us to ponder those questions that push us to grow.

The story line in the song depicts the main character escaping into a dream to avoid the pain of the loss of the woman he loves, a dream of a spring landscape bursting with color, flowers, meadows, and bird songs. In the dream a rooster crows, and our hero awakes to hear more sinister birds, ravens, harbingers of death, shrieking on the rooftop. In his semiconscious state he thinks the wintry ice crystals on the window are flowers and allows himself to fall once more into a pleasant dream, now one of requited love. Once again the roosters crow and he awakes with beating heart to the cold reality.

James O., once a student of Ben's and now a professional singer, has come back to Ben Zander's class with his pianist for coaching in this song. Ben's job, as always, is to create the conditions that support the artist to become a pathway, a conduit through which the listener's body and spirit can attune with the universe. To establish a platform for James, Ben shares the story of the song so that the artists and the audience are brought together into an understanding of the setting, the tradition, and the plot. Ben comes to the nineteenth-century German art songs, or *Lieder*, via his love and knowledge of literature, and it is probably what makes him such an effective teacher in this genre.

Through his formative years, Ben was apprenticed to the great Spanish cellist, Gaspar Cassadó, whose footsteps he was slated to follow onto the concert stage. However, when Ben transitioned to a full-size cello and from gut strings to steel strings, he discovered that his fingers were unable to make the calluses that are necessary to make a career as a professional cellist, and he simply couldn't continue. In the wake of this trauma, at the age of twenty-one he returned to London and took up English literature at the University of London. From his literary studies, Ben received a Harkness Fellowship to come to Boston. Once in Boston, he was asked to substitute as a cello teacher for a friend at the New England Conservatory. That led to a job conducting at a summer music camp and then employment as the conductor of the Civic Symphony of Boston. What a strange and lucky sequence of events—not without its distressing aspects, of course. But how much richer is his understanding of music and his teaching (and conducting!) for that rerouting of his path.

Ben tells the class that in the German poetic tradition, Nature and the human heart are inextricably linked. Nature is a projection of a human being's thoughts. How else but through art can one embody those ideas?

The piano and the voice begin, James singing gorgeously. At the point in the text where the hero awakes to crows on the roof, the piano comes in with a loud harsh chord, but James seems to take no notice. "Stop," says Ben, "this isn't opera. This is Lieder. Lieder is never about your voice, it's about your feelings. Turn your attention to what's happened here. There is a bird screaming overhead. The hero is confused. There are flowers on the window made of ice. James, pay attention! This is not a showcase for a star. Don't sing. Dream. It's *never* about your voice."

Some of the most memorable musical performances are those by past artists that we are able to hear only through the faulty technology of decades ago, where hardly anything but the musicality comes through—I'm referring to those scratchy performances on acoustical 78s of Enrico Caruso, Melba, Fritz Kreisler, and Paderewski. It takes an artist willing to participate fully in the present moment, conscious of what the composer intends, aware of what his pianist is doing, and what his heart tells him, to forgo the deliciousness of looking so good. And looking good, as you will recognize, is one of mankind's favorite survival patterns.

Ben turns toward the class. "There is always something precise in the narrative in Schubert. It's on the level of detail of the hero thinking, 'I want to get back into the dream but my heart is beating so hard that I can't do it.' You have to know what is being said at every moment and understand the complexity of it. Then you will know that you can't launch into opera. You have to deal in your singing with the ambiguity and the poignancy.

"Now here," he says, pointing to the score, "Schubert comes along with the hardest question of all: 'When will the flowers on the window become green again? When will I hold my loved one in my arms?' But we know neither will ever, ever happen. How do you sing that? How does the singer convey both the hope and the knowledge that there is no hope?"

As we have seen, it is those out-of-the-ordinary moments of

emotional intensity that leave us ripe for change. Music mimics nature as a living evolution in real time, and if the musicians and the audience are attuned on all levels, it is possible to feel integration happening in the moment that allows us to take a new step into unknown territory.

> Occasionally one sees something fleeting in the land, a moment when line, color, and movement intensify and something sacred is revealed, leading one to believe that there is another realm of reality corresponding to the physical one, but different.*

HANDIWORK OF THE HEART

Perhaps the most important thing we have learned so far is that if we shift our attention away from what we think we want, and put it on what our hearts tell us *life* wants, we will find ourselves extremely powerful in creating the conditions and connections that were missing. It seems that we may also find ourselves held in the rich sense of community we may implicitly long for.

The following is the story of a man who boldly took on Nature's processes on her own turf, or to follow our earlier analogy, in her own shoes, offering himself and his technology to her with the utmost intelligence and respect. By so doing he was led to witness, under his own hands, life at its most miraculous, and so will we.

The story goes that while working as a forest researcher in East Kalimantan, Indonesia, in 1989, where half of the primary forest has been destroyed through clear-cutting, Dr. Willie Smits and his wife were walking around an outdoor market and met the gaze of a baby orangutan peering out of a cage. The baby orangutan, said

---

* Barry Lopez, *Arctic Dreams: Imagination and Desire in a Northern Landscape* (New York: Vintage Books, 2001), 274.

Willie Smits, had the saddest eyes he had ever seen. Later, in the night, Dr. Smits returned to look for the caged baby and found its body thrown on a rubbish heap, still barely alive, the cage gone. He took the infant orangutan home, rubbed its belly, made it drink, and nursed it back to health. Word got around and people began bringing other displaced, hurt, or abandoned orangutans to his care. The work that he started there of rescuing, rehabilitating, and releasing orangutans into the wild developed into what became the Borneo Orangutan Survival Foundation.

To save the orangutans, Dr. Smits realized that the priority had to be restoring their forest habitats, and to do that he had to return economic security to the local people, whose only means of livelihood was reduced to what they gained from cutting down trees. With the backing of the Borneo Orangutan Survival Foundation, he leaped into one of the most ambitious reforestation projects ever conceived, rebuilding a completely devastated rain forest of 2,000 hectares (7.7 square miles) where at the start no rain fell, no species lived, no birds sang, no industry took hold, and the local people spent 22 percent of their meager resources just to get enough water to survive.

Much of the area's deforestation was due to the planting of oil palms for Western biofuels, disrupting miles of peat bogs that let go so much CO_2 that Borneo is, at the date of this writing, the world's third greatest emitter of greenhouse gases after China and the United States.

Willie took on his project with a vengeance. "My idea was," he says, "if I can do this in the worst possible place I can think of where there is really nothing left, no one will have an excuse to say, 'Yeah, but . . .'"

His intent was to create a set of recipes to restore what man has destroyed, and in Samboja Lestari, a small village in Borneo, the first steps were to acquire the land from the locals. The plan was to pay some families outright for their property, or to give them land within the restoration area to grow food for their families in exchange for their help in rebuilding and protecting the forest. "What

I really did," Dr. Smits says, "I just followed nature." First they planted low-yield acacia trees along with many other types of trees for diversity that in a few years' time would produce timber, then they ringed the five thousand acres with a thick thorny hedge to provide protection for the orangutans for whom they made a sanctuary in the center. Next they planted biofuel-rich sugar palms all along the edge—a completely different tree from the oil palm whose monoculture had destroyed the area. The sugar palms would be able, within six years, to provide plenty of income to support and sustain the local people.

The recipe for the middle region was first to plant pineapples, beans, and corn; in the second phase, bananas and papayas, later on chocolate and chilies so that the people would always have some food and some income. Then slowly the trees that were planted first would take over and bring in fruits and timber and fuel wood. Finally the sugar palm forest would flourish and provide people with permanent income. Sugar palms thrive only in a diverse forest, so they had no chance when Dr. Smits and his native team began. But once the other trees took root, the sugar palms grew to stand as protective sentinels for the whole project: they are fire and flood resistant, need no fertilizer, are champion photosynthesizers, and because of their deep roots, they enrich the soil around them. Each tree is tapped two or three times a day for its abundant juice, which can be made into sugar products and ethanol for fuel and electricity.

"A natural forest has many layers on the ground and above, so I followed nature's plan as closely as I could," says Smits. "We grow fast-growing trees and then slow growing of high diversity, and the right fungi that brings nourishment back to the trees." The fungi turned out to be a far more critical part of the ecosystem than Smits at first understood.

Education of the people is a crucial step in this recipe for transformation, just as it was a necessary part of Nalini Nadkarni's, and Ben Zander's. Dr. Smits introduced the villagers to the many aspects of the life cycle of a forest, and to new technologies to monitor growth; and as they learned they developed a proprietary feeling for every aspect of the project. They planted thousands of trees, Smits says, representing ten times the variety of species in all of Europe.

At the three-year mark, rain was again able to form above Samboja Lestari because in this type of ecosystem it is the leaves of trees that call forth the rain. The clear-cutting had produced an ecosystem that was dry, overheated, and inhospitable to life of any kind. But in a mere thirty-six months of careful and cooperative reforesting, temperatures had dropped approximately eight to ten degrees Fahrenheit, and the preserve that had been almost devoid of life was home once again to 137 species of birds and 30 species of reptiles.

At four years, the climate in Samboja Lestari had changed in every way (who says it can't be done?). Fires and floods were no longer threats, the temperature and humidity had become life supporting, biodiversity was vastly increased, and where once the land was burned and scarred, now all you could see from the air was green. At this point Willie Smits gave the people back the land he had bought from them. In addition, at this four-year mark, Samboja Lestari was supporting three thousand jobs. The people deeply understand, says Smits, that their lives depend on the forest, and each village had designed its own unique way of assuring that everyone cooperates, so that no one in their midst cuts down prohibited trees or violates in any way the plan for the forest.

A few years later, Dr. Smits invented a compact, portable palm sugar processor that can be dropped into the most remote village by helicopter. The little factory is, like nature, a no-waste operation making sugar and ethanol, with by-products of algae for animal food and fertilizer, and by a filtering process, clean air and clean water. Now the cycle is complete: the forest and the people take care of each other in a richly sustainable way, the children are being educated, and the orangutans, the impetus for the entire project, enjoy a protected life in the center of it all.

CHAPTER TWENTY-SIX

The Territory Beyond

W E'VE COME TO A new territory—the Territory Beyond—beyond what we know and expect of ourselves as human beings, beyond the norms of achievement or psychology, beyond our ordinary measures of happiness, and beyond what we picture as vitality. Let's say that in this territory the distinction between what it is that *we* want and what *life* wants fades and ultimately disappears. We feel whole and in tune and easily imagine that we are resonating with the shimmering oscillations of the very energy fields of the earth itself. Grateful for Nature's collaborative presence, we deem ourselves to be joyfully capable of all we can imagine.

In case you haven't already figured out the location of the Territory Beyond, let me give you one more indication. You can't get there all by yourself, because in truth there is no such thing as a human being by herself. We don't exist alone. Having the thought

189

of one other being, seeing one point of light on the opposite shore, remembering one song of love is enough to animate you and prepare you to dwell in the Territory. As you may have guessed, what we are calling the Territory Beyond is located inside *you* where all of creation resides.

When you have found your way into the fertile expanse of the Territory, you may discover that your every deed sends ripples throughout the cosmos. You can feel them because, after all, they are rippling through the universe in you. This Territory, always at hand, might be described as a deeper level of reality than we are familiar with, one that is more malleable than we believe life to be from our habit of thinking in compartments. Here, friends know things about each other at a distance, and electrons are in rotational step on opposite sides of our galaxy. In the Territory Beyond, mind and matter are felt as one, which means that we will fare best if we are quite disciplined in what we say and intend. After all, as we have come to understand, the story we are living into manifests in one way or another as the life we live.

There is a "wormhole" I would recommend to you through which you can slip to find yourself wholly centered in the Territory Beyond. It takes an adult mind to locate it, one that is open, curious, and creative, and willing to have its worldview overthrown by an experience of the miraculous. You enter by committing to a game, or exploration of a certain sort. Commitment is the operative word, because the kind of game I am suggesting has its own set of rules that may be antithetical to what you might feel like doing in any given moment. I may be skating on thin ice here, because many people would describe a religious practice in just those terms. Insofar as a person commits to living by certain prescribed guidelines and that commitment carries him over hardship and brings him into peace, harmony, and ecstasy, the process has similarities. The difference in most cases is that the games I am describing have no dualism to them, no "good" and no "evil," no higher power from whose grace one can fall. These are not games at which you can fail; you simply engage without reservation, without knowing the outcome.

The field of the Territory Beyond highlights experiences other than winning or losing: the surprise and pleasure of seeing the world anew, for instance, of knowing oneself as a contribution, of love radiating from and around you, and of extraordinary accomplishment where it is not clear to you that you are the doer. So you are likely to find yourself expanding into these states, even if they were not, for you, a reason for playing.

Consider the following story of Sir Ernest Shackleton, who went on a literal exploration that turned into a test of the power of the mind to defy the odds of accepted reality.

OPTIMISM IS THE TRUE MORAL COURAGE

It started when Shackleton posted this advertisement to enlist a crew to make the very first crossing of the Antarctic continent: "Men wanted for hazardous journey. Small wages. Bitter cold. Long months of complete darkness. Constant danger. Safe return doubtful. Honour and recognition (only) in case of success." We can view Shackleton's proposed venture as a game of exploration, with clearly stated parameters likely to draw only the most fearless among men. Pulling no punches, the ad was an all-out challenge to commit.

The journey was indeed hazardous. Leaving from Plymouth, England, on August 6, 1914, the *Endurance* arrived in the waters of South Georgia Island, east of the Antarctic Peninsula, on November 5. A month later, on December 5, she headed south along the coast of Antarctica, but almost immediately encountered soft but dense polar ice. With only two hundred miles to go to Vahsel Bay, where Shackleton planned to meet a second ship, the *Aurora*, to complete his expedition, he and his crew persevered in slowly working their way through the frozen waters of the Weddell Sea.

However, by January 24, as winds and gales pressed the ice against the land, the *Endurance* became trapped in the pack ice. Notwithstanding their heroic efforts the crew was unable to free the vessel, and after ten months—nearly a year!—of patiently waiting for a thaw, the pressure of the ice finally crushed the ship. Shackleton and his men were then stranded on the ice floes, where they camped for five more months, enduring unimaginable hardships, waiting to drift to open water. When they were finally able to make passage, they sailed the three small lifeboats they had salvaged to a spare expanse of rocky land devoid of human habitation called Elephant Island, far from any hope of rescue.

Faced with a crew who were strained to the limit, physically, mentally, and emotionally, Shackleton acted quickly. He took five men and immediately set out in a twenty-two-foot lifeboat on an impossible eight-hundred-mile journey through the world's worst seas at the very worst time of the year. They aimed for the nearest populated territory, South Georgia Island and its whaling station, from whence the *Endurance* had embarked a year and a half earlier.

Miraculously, the six men found their way to the back side of South Georgia Island and landed on a stark, uninhabited rocky coast, then had to cross twenty-six miles of mountains and glaciers, considered impassable, to reach the settlement on the other side. Shackleton took two men with him to make the journey, climbing and backtracking over high snow-covered passes to the station, arriving in such an emaciated form as to be almost unrecognizable as human beings.

In August 1916, nearly twenty-two months after the initial departure of the *Endurance*, Shackleton himself returned in a seaworthy boat to rescue the men on Elephant Island. Though they had suffered injury, infection, hypothermia, attacks by an elephant seal, near starvation, and unspeakable conditions, not one member of the original twenty-eight-man crew was lost.

How was this possible? We have meager clues, but one stands out. Shackleton remained consistently positive in his outlook, and he forbade the expression of negativity or despair. "Optimism is the true moral courage," he declared, and he led his men accordingly. If we think of the journey of the *Endurance* as an "engagement" similar to a game, the instructions were "Commit to life whole-heartedly with every fiber of your being, in your speaking and your actions."

Shackleton knew, and so did his first mate Frank Wild, that the discipline required was not a matter of behavior. It was not like observing a schedule of doing twenty push-ups a day. The discipline was in the narrative, in keeping the story straight. There could be no room for any other story, because the story of the poor odds of surviving would almost inevitably kill the men. In this game, death as an option was off the table.

Frank Wild was left behind in charge of the twenty-two remaining men on Elephant Island for more than four months, without the slightest reason to *believe* that Shackleton and the others would ever return, and without any means of escape to safety. At the moment when the group witnessed their captain and his five men set off for South Georgia Island in their open rowboat, Wild reported, "We gave them three hearty cheers and watched the boat getting smaller and smaller in the distance. Then seeing some of the party in tears, I immediately set them all to work." "You see, boss," said one of the men to their captain when it was all over, "Wild never gave up hope, and whenever the sea was at all clear of ice he rolled up his sleeping-bag and said to all hands, 'Roll up your sleeping-bags, boys; the boss may come to-day.'"

In his 1974 book, *The Medusa and the Snail*, Lewis Thomas, scientist and consummate observer, describes how a mouse, caught in the jaws of a cat, goes limp when it sees that "the jig is up," and endorphins, those feel-good chemicals, flood its body, easing its way into death. It was crucial that not one of those twenty-eight men should under any circumstances indulge in the enticing narrative that the jig was up, or that death was nigh. Not a single man could enjoy the release that giving up would have brought. To save their collective lives it was imperative that each one maintain his optimism about making it through. There is a great deal of research that confirms that the kinds of positive feelings involved in keeping up belief in a good outcome have a strengthening effect on the immune system and on the energetic output of our hearts to people around us. Brain cells, too, synchronize their activity with the brains of others when they want to link up. "The cells literally tune into each other's wavelength," says Laura Colgin of the Kavli Institute for Systems Neuroscience in Trondheim, Norway, thereby fortifying their hosts and turning many into one aligned intention. In following their instructions so faithfully, the men on Elephant Island seem to have fallen into collective resonance. When one man tripped and spilled his precious allotment of milk, the account goes, his cup was seamlessly filled by donations from the starving others.

In all likelihood, Sir Ernest Shackleton did not perceive the voyage of the *Endurance* as a game in any trivial sense, but his continued good spirits, and openness to both adventure and risk, certainly would have qualified him as being "game." When the expedition came to an end he wrote, "We had 'suffered, starved and triumphed, groveled down yet grasped at glory, grown bigger in the bigness of the whole.' We had seen God in His splendours, heard the text that Nature renders. We had reached the naked soul of man."

INFINITE GAMES

In his seminal book *Finite and Infinite Games*, professor emeritus of history and literature at NYU James Carse distinguishes two types of games. The first is the kind we are most familiar with where there is an objective, rules for getting there, and a chance to be a winner. Soccer and Monopoly are included in this group, as are corporate year-end goals with their promise of bonuses. Carse calls this type of game a "finite game" because it has an end point, usually when one person or team succeeds ahead of others. The second type is a game where there are no winners or losers, and no defined end, only an inspiring purpose. Carse names these games "infinite games." For example, Ben's father-in-law used to practice the viola and my mother studied Russian, both well into their eighties, for no other reason but the pleasure of the discipline. Cree Native Americans recommend that each day one learn and teach one meaningful thing, perform a small act of mercy, and treat all living things with respect. Their practices would all qualify as infinite games where winning and losing are replaced by "the integrity of the effort." Finite games, Carse says, will progressively wear out our souls, partly because for a game of winning and losing you must always prove yourself to an audience, but infinite games will only energize us. Infinite players have no serious agenda, but are "the joyful poets of a story that continues to originate from what they cannot finish." The history of art and the history of science are records of work that is never finished but serves as a platform for others to continue and build upon. Infinite players are evolutionary. Ultimately, "there is but one infinite game," Carse says, as he ends his book, and we know that that is life itself.

GAMES FROM THE ACCOMPLISHMENT GROUP

When I have offered assignments to people over the years, I have called them by different names: explorations, engagements, adventures, and games, depending on the context. "Assignments" works well for students; "explorations" is just right for those who wish only to be Sunday afternoon players; "adventures" is an active invitation for people to stretch out into new terrains; "engagements" is a warm, lighthearted term for use among friends; and "games" by itself connotes commitment and rules of play, but runs the risk of sounding trivial. So in my own mind, when I use any of the above terms I am including all the qualities that the brilliant James Carse refers to when he writes of "infinite games": commitment, far-reaching adventure, unlimited extension, and the joy of play. I hope they resonate in yours.

The following games are my strategy to take us further into the unknown and promote our growth, and that's why I am devoting so much room to them in this chapter. They were a staple of an accomplishment program I started years ago, wherein participants signed up with a project they were committed to accomplishing over the eight months of the program. We worked both in a linear structure, which included steps, goals, and measures, and in parallel in a nonlinear fashion. For instance, at the end of each session I offered a new infinite game for the attendees to play and report on in the next meeting. The games generally required the players to take an intuitive leap. One of the first assignments was the instruction to "Get in Touch with Someone Who Is Lost to You." The players soon discovered that a powerful way to identify who, or what, was lost was to let their minds drift until an answer floated up, similar to the process I use when I consult Altair in his forest aerie.

One man, Joe, came to remember a misunderstanding with his college roommate fifteen years prior. They had been very close, but a feeling of injury had kept Joe from making any contact since. Although he was nervous about addressing the issue, Joe was a committed player and knew what he had to do once he had located his friend. The next weekend he boarded an airplane and went from Boston to Colorado to visit him. The issue stemmed from a miscommunication that was easily cleared up, leaving the two men eager to camp out in the desert under the stars and catch up with each other's lives, renewing the friendship that had simply gone underground intact. Another participant, Helen, came to the conclusion that it was a part of herself that she had lost, and she restarted the music lessons that she had dropped ten years before. For one group member, the startling realization was that it was her husband with whom she lived on a daily basis who was lost to her. When she came to the next meeting she told us a moving story of intimacy rekindled. All of the players registered a little shock of surprise at identifying the person or thing that was lost to them, being quite unconscious of the fact that someone or something was waiting to be found.

An open-ended engagement like this can be played on any level, as you can see; you can step right up to the plate and get on an airplane, or you can do something simpler, like take your patiently waiting dog for a really long walk. If you don't shrink from it, your unconscious will tell you what will serve you best. A man in one of my groups didn't react at first to this assignment, but six months later sought out his teenage birth child with whom he had had no contact since her earliest days. We in the group had no idea that he was a father, that's how lost to each other they were.

Try exploring this yourself, or do so with a friend. If you even consider it, the rich field of your unconscious mind will deliver your assignment to you. Don't ignore it. Step into it with moral courage, in other words, wholeheartedly, and with a sense of possibility. The next game on the list I used in that program is "Get the Love You Want." Do you want to let your unconscious tackle that?

There is another open-ended game that I am particularly fond of. It functions like a towrope to pull you out of your habitual decision-making patterns. In a broad sense, those patterns identify you as who you are, and are likely to be fractals of the habits of people in your past, so this exploration can initiate a multigenerational transformation. It is played like this: you pick one of the following qualities to use as your guiding principle, the way Shackleton's men lived by optimism, but for a much more limited span of time!

Wonder
Desire
Service
Authenticity
Vitality
Lightness
Courage

The instructions for this game are:

Pick one of these qualities and commit to making every decision in line with that choice over one to three days.

At each decision point, whether it be choosing stocks or choosing socks, or speaking to a colleague, you ask yourself (depending on which one you signed up for), "What is the courageous choice? Or what is it I really desire?" Or, "What conversation do I have if I am living a life of service?" Write the word on your person because it is easy to forget what you are doing. Include choices from the smallest to the most consequential. See where the game takes you. Once the game is in play, stay with the quality you chose.

The criterion for the qualities is that they be of absolute value. Substituting "Control" won't do, nor will "Being the Best," or "Living Up to Your Potential." As you can imagine, a number of people around you would not appreciate the competition and constriction you would be exhibiting, were you to choose guidelines like those. This is a game that by definition leaves no one down or out in your wake!

COURAGE

I made my test run of this infinite game by undertaking a solo three-day skiing weekend. I stuck a piece of tape on the back of my glove, printed with the word COURAGE in bold red marker. I was determined to take the courageous route at every choice point, with a dream to sail effortlessly down runs labeled with black diamonds by the end of the weekend. (I considered myself an advanced beginner at best—even the word "advanced" as a modifier for "beginner" felt daring for me.) I was excited both about skiing and about playing my new game, but not at all convinced that anything much would happen. After a breakfast of poached eggs (I was squeamish about them), and after zipping myself into a suit

that made me look both unflatteringly wide and way too professional (it took courage), I started my exploration.

In the lift line I hesitated, then stepped forward with some mental effort to impose upon the person in front of me. As we rode the
lift together, we chatted. I asked him his skiing level ("Are you
crazy?" I thought; "You're going to have to answer the same question"), and when the question came to me I took the courageous
leap: "Intermediate," I said—not a lie, merely a stretch. As we slid
off the lift, I yearned to follow the trail marked by the green square,
but given our conversation (and my commitment) I felt I must take
the blue route, and it turned out that I could manage it perfectly
well.

I created quite a challenge out of lunch. I opted to go to an expensive restaurant in town, still in my suit, and ordered the most
disturbing thing on the menu. Then I actually ate it, while I en-
dured the gaze of customers eyeing the woman stuffed into bib and
pants, dining on tripe, alone.

By the afternoon the sun had melted the snow and the slopes
were shining with ice. Fear gripped my legs, and I toppled, again
and again, suffering the ignominy of the struggle to return to my
feet. I was about to quit this game in well-reasoned defeat, but
glanced at the word, stuck to my glove, recalling my intention.
COURAGE.

Next, a flash of insight. I saw that my entire body was behaving
as though the ice were an impediment to skiing, whereas in New
England, ice is just about as common as snow. Skiing *is* skiing on
ice—almost by definition.

The revelation blew my mind (fortunately) and my body relaxed. I went straight over the ice, allowing gravity to carry me. At
the bottom, I registered disbelief. How could it be that I had just
navigated those icy slopes? I thought for a moment and realized I
hadn't navigated anything, I had just allowed gravity to carry me
down, while I got myself out of the way. This new, less heroic,
more collaborative image began to inform my view of myself, and

I took to the mountain again, now a more easygoing skier. I asked some people I met in the lift line to join me for dinner that evening, and we had a great time with plenty to talk about.

By the morning of the third day, I felt wild, rapturous, and free! I "gravitated" toward the young and strapping and rode the lifts with them. I shared my game, and joined their flock, and yes, on this last day these expert skiers and I virtually flew down the black diamond slopes, like fledgling swallows in transit between heaven and earth.

I was, to say the least, stunned. Three days prior, I had devised a game and set out to do a hitherto untested experiment. I stuck with it, and everything turned topsy-turvy. On Friday I was a hesitant, self-doubting, middle-aged woman only barely able to call myself an "advanced beginner" on skis, and I became by the end of Sunday a self-confident member of a group of youthful skiers, feeling myself to be half my age. I actually admired my image, initially a source of humiliation, in the mirror in the lodge. I relished icy surfaces. I was now convinced that gravity, the group, and most of all, the game would take care of everything—I was not the "doer" anymore. I remember standing at the bottom of the mountain, shaking my head and saying, "Things are not as they seem." Events don't happen as we assume they do, by effort and will applied step by step. No, life isn't like that. I had stepped into a new story, a new field, and all that was required of me to reach my goal was to take the courageous option at every turn. Hardly any of my actions were ones I would have ordinarily taken. I was under the sway of the context, of the field, of the story.

LIGHTNESS

Allow me to have a little fun with you for a moment. Granting myself a gift for precognition, I am going to describe what will happen for you when you opt to play this game and choose the quality "Lightness."

The first ten things that go wrong in your day you will later see are part of basic training. You get nervous when you realize you've run out of coffee, convinced you will not be up to the challenges ahead. In the spirit of the game, you declare with false cheer, "Oh, I'll do fine." And then you are amused to notice that you feel, well, *fine*. The newspaper informs you that the terror alert level is up to orange. After the stomach tightening, and the habitual internal argument—"What are we supposed to DO about it, for heaven's sake?"—you say lightly, "Thanks for sharing," and pat the newspaper fondly. You are amused at how well you feel. But by noon you are in a foul mood. You are still unable to rouse your son, just back from his graduation from college. You see the summer stretching out drearily ahead, day turning into night, no job, no productivity, his chances of success slipping away. As you hold on to the newel post and shout up the stairs, you glimpse the word you have written on a piece of masking tape stuck to your arm, LIGHTNESS. "How the *@%* do I deal with THIS lightly?!" Only remembering the word "Commit" allows you to stay the course.

You begin to lighten up when you have a brief moment of clarity: Your son is blissfully sleeping the day away in his childhood room (free of charge, of course), and you, though shouting noisily, are keeping forever silent on the subject of what you want from him. So he might as well be thirteen years old, and you might as well be the parent of a young teen, the way you are acting, asking nothing of him and bellowing up the stairs. The humor in it doesn't escape you. You suddenly don't care whether he appears at all today, making a mental note to work it out with him sometime when you are both awake. You call a friend and suggest meeting for a light lunch.

When you extend the game beyond basic training, miracles appear like fireflies. Tasks that you traditionally viewed as onerous you carry out easily, and with a light step, because you *can*. It is the simplest thing in the world. People around you seem to "hear" you better, so you don't have to shout and become emphatic. You develop a light step, a light touch, light in the eyes, and you begin to take yourself lightly. Even the cloudy weather is enlivening to you because it is . . . so completely *itself*.

You give up all efforts at control—you walk by your daughter's clothes spread from one end of the house to the other, and let them be. In another moment, you put on some inspiring music and wash every dish in the sink.

The "you" of the stationary world—right-minded, coercive, and domineering—takes on cartoon form, and you keep popping up as your own favorite joke. From this ebullient place, a desire is hardly out of your mouth before the world starts to shift and change to accommodate it. "Let's revitalize the ocean!" you declare cheerfully. Your son, that son who was never going to get out of bed, appears in the doorway, still sleepy, and tells you he has an interview tomorrow for an internship at the state senator's Office of Environmental Affairs.

PLAYING WITH THE OTHER FIVE

So let me recommend to you that if you want some energy and want to have more fun, try taping "vitality" to your sleeve, and transform difficult phone calls, messy rooms, or any old tired issue into a vibrant encounter. If you opt for "authenticity" you'll be likely to run into an old colleague or a past lover on the street, and this time you won't pretend you haven't seen her. And when, after a brief conversation, you part, you well may have a new relationship and a deeper understanding of yourself. If you are often plagued by thoughts of what you are missing in life, you might take up the quality "service" and make every choice about assisting others. Perhaps life will take on a different meaning, or maybe you will discover how complete your life really is. If you commit to "wonder," time may stretch out luxuriously while you stand mesmerized by a baby's smile or see the beauty in ordinary events; your family coming together for dinner, for instance, or a breeze rippling through the trees. If you are so weighted down with "reality" that you never know what you want, then spend a few days living by the principle of "desire." You'll begin to get the hang of it when you find yourself boosting the volume on iTunes, insisting that your dog become well mannered, or ordering a thousand daffodil bulbs for planting in the fall.

I have a further suggestion: Put something spectacular at stake, the achievement of which will spin you outside the limits of luck and stationary reality. Then choose one of the qualities, any one, and play the game. See whether all of nature itself lines up behind you.

PART IV

A Pack

of Games

I have chosen to offer, at greater length, five infinite games that I feel have relevance for almost any moment of our everyday lives. As you take them up, you will be continually changing the context of your life, who you say you are, and how you view the world by the moves you make and the transformations you undergo. May you travel far, if only deep into your own backyard.

"Mind is not a thing but a process—the very process of life. In other words, the organizing activity of living systems, at all levels of life, is mental activity. The interactions of a living organism—plant, animal, or human—with its environment are cognitive, or mental interactions. . . ."

Fritjof Capra, *The Web of Life*

There Is All the Time in the World

W E KNOW THAT THE workplace is eager to convince people that they can and should get more done in less time, work fast and lean, and produce greater results. How can one argue with the principle, even if it doesn't always turn out the way we want it to? Who would believe you if you countered this received wisdom and declared that people should relax, because "there is all the time in the world"? Anyway, what does it mean?

It's a story, of course, one that is designed to rewire the way we think about Time. Currently our concept of "time" is something akin to a Swiss railroad train running along a track and showing up at precise intervals—always on time, of course. While this concretization of the passage of time gives us an important means of coordinating our activities, it also focuses our attention on the regular pulse of the clock to the detriment of altogether different sets of rhythms: the rhythm of speaking that communicates best, or our optimal, individual rhythm for getting things done, or the rhythm at which our unconscious mind processes information, or the rhythms of the life and people around us.

The Swiss train model implies that we are traveling on a straight track relentlessly toward a next station. No wonder we cry out that there are not enough hours in the day for us to do all the things we feel we must do; no wonder we often want to stop the train so we can catch our breath. But of course there really isn't a straight track or an inevitable next station. All there is is the expanding and contracting ever-elastic *Now* of which we all partake. When you feel stressed and breathless perhaps it signifies that you are out of resonance with powerful natural rhythms, the ones that will cooperate with you to get what you want to get done, easily, in flow. Perhaps it means that you are falsely elevating yourself to the status of chief actor, using your insignificant will to push things through and oblivious to the interactive system around you.

The game with no goal and no limits, called "there is all the time in the world," has the power to get you back in step, to bring you back to your center, to connect you once more with a universe that will be your partner. To embark on an exploration of this terrain you simply say to yourself, when you are feeling dominated by the pressure of time, "There is all the time in the world, you know," and you take a deep breath and sigh. If what "wants to happen" aligns with what you want to accomplish, I wager it will get done well and with ease.

I first played this game one Thanksgiving Day when all the relatives and one or two friends were coming to my house for dinner. I planned first to clean, then to buy any forgotten groceries, bread, and flowers with a reminder to pick up candles, then to create a beautiful table, and get that turkey in early enough. I realized I had to fashion a makeshift rack for the bird, which I hadn't counted on, and then mash the potatoes, coordinate the cooking of asparagus and Brussels sprouts, get the wine into newly empty spaces in the fridge when the other dishes came out, set out what is needed to make gravy, and bathe and dress, and then put out appetizers and glasses, light a fire, and greet the family with enthusiasm and attention. To the mind of a quasi-perfectionist the next few hours would be, predictably, an overwhelming and anxiety-producing effort.

"There's all the time in the world, you know. Time for everything," I intoned to myself. I took that breath, let out a sigh, and went about the business of creating Thanksgiving from an alternate universe, one of presence and ease. I had such a good time! I got to arrange a gorgeous table with flowers I had picked out one by one, listen to music as I snapped the ends of the asparagus, exercise creative zeal in inventing a device to elevate the turkey made out of perforated aluminum foil held up by river stones, and again and again taste the sweet potatoes for the right amount of sherry until I felt a lovely buzz. I was smiling all morning and doing everything at a leisurely pace, barely looking at the clock. I thought to myself, "This is a great Thanksgiving Day even if no one comes and we never get to dinner." But they did come, and I was relaxed and ready and so glad to see them, and all the while I marveled at the simple but momentous shift that occurred when I played the game "there is time for everything—all the time in the world."

There was one trip that Ben and I made to South Africa where our three-week timetable was arranged entirely for us by an enlightened woman named Louise van Rhyn and her company, Symphonia. When we arrived we found out that she had scheduled ninety-three events for us over twenty-one days, and not small events, at that. They included large-scale performances of several hours in duration, a two-day coaching workshop, group work with women who were starting businesses, and presentations to many different groups: to two business schools, as well as to two sets of youth leaders, to elementary school teachers, and to several music groups. There were dinners at which we were expected to perform and an orchestra concert where Ben conducted the Beethoven Ninth—even a presentation in front of Parliament. Four more events were added over the three weeks, totaling ninety-seven! When we looked at the list of them, we declared that this was impossible, but once we got going my concept of what was possible changed radically, especially in relation to time. It was on that trip that I began to say, "There's all the time in the world, you know," and deeply mean it.

One evening after dark, members of our team were on our way from different parts of Cape Town in separate taxis to a radio station where we were to be broadcast live at 9:00 p.m. It was nearing 8:30. My driver didn't have directions to the station, and was quite worried because he really had no idea how to get there. His dispatcher wasn't helpful, cutting in via the car radio and shouting at him angrily that he had to get me to the station on time and that he should use the GPS on his phone. But just then the battery on the driver's phone went dead so we had to stop at a 7-Eleven store to get a new one, and when he came out of the store he was even more agitated. From the backseat I put my hand on his shoulder and said, "Don't worry, there is all the time in the world," and as I said it I laughed and felt very relaxed, and slowly his shoulder relaxed as well. I repeated the phrase unhurriedly and with good humor a couple of times and we got there on time! Actually we were the first ones to arrive, in advance of the two other cabs.

I found myself using the phrase in several other circumstances during those three weeks. One was on the way to the two-day coaching workshop, and although the driver knew the destination, muddy roads and flooding slowed us down and threatened to make us late. When this driver began to show tension, I told him there was nothing to worry about because there was all the time in the world, and again I felt very calm. I looked up at the sky at that moment and saw that we were driving into a huge rainbow. (Permit me the pleasure of linking the two.) It was smooth sailing from then on, and although we arrived a few minutes late, it made no difference at all.

Time is too slow for those who wait, too swift for those who fear, too long for those who grieve, too short for those who rejoice, but for those who love, time is eternity.

HENRY VAN DYKE, AMERICAN AUTHOR, EDUCATOR, AND
CLERGYMAN (1852–1933)

This game will make lovers of us all.

Walk with Spirit and Love

I'M NOT SURE YOUR mother meant "Walk with spirit and love" when she admonished you to stand up straight, although she may have had a bit of this practice in mind. It is true that posture changes your outlook, lifts your spirits, and when you stand up straight you make a good, confident presentation. But we are talking about something both more radical and more fundamental here. This is an exploration that will create a bridge to the Territory Beyond where you are no longer an individual making it on your own; rather where you feel a compelling connectivity to everything around you.

We might ask before we begin, "What is meant by Spirit? What is meant by Love?" You may have to answer that for yourself, but when I think of Spirit, I think of it as a glowing aura around us that draws us to stand tall and radiate happiness. I think of it as the spark that instantly connects us. And I think of Spirit as limitless in sight and wisdom. Love, on the other hand, is much more visceral for me, a warm energy that centers in the heart, runs throughout the body, and suffuses my world.

You'll notice that the game stipulates that you walk *with* Spirit and Love. It doesn't say walk *as*, or walk *informed by.* That little preposition "with" gives the game a double meaning. One definition has it that you are to radiate Spirit and Love from your own being, and another pictures you accompanied by the figures of Spirit and Love personified. The three of you make a powerful, high-spirited team so you, buoyed up, are not doing it all on your own.

Notice also that the rules of this game require more of you or your team than that you stand and radiate; they ask you to change your location as you do so. The directions say *walk*, so move, be energetic in bringing Spirit and Love to the world. So now try it: stand up and walk with Spirit and Love, and if you need a boost of energy turn to Spirit on your right and nod or wink, and if you want to widen your heart turn to your left, smile, and let in the warmth of Love.

MIRACULOUS SHIFTS

I assign these games-without-limit in a number of settings as an experiment that will produce data on their transformational value. A recent Harvard graduate, now living in Korea, praised this game for having opened doors for her in a culture she found so different from her own. She describes how being unfamiliar with the Korean language had prevented her from properly communicating warmth and acceptance with those she met. But, she says, "Walk with Spirit and Love" means you start out with love, you don't wait for a sign that you are accepted. Coming from love generates love. "Walking with love is now as much a matter of survival as it is part of my mission to make the most of the blessings I have been given in life."

Here is a report from another woman who received "Walk with Spirit and Love" as an assignment in an accomplishment group.

Weeks later, she held the room still with the wonder of what had happened for her in taking it up:

> I was asked to sing at the wake of a person whom I did not know personally. I agreed to do it as a favor, but I didn't realize what a production the event would be. I was in a very negative mood when I arrived, I'll have to admit, and it was very hot and the heat and the sheer number of people crowding into the room where the wake was in progress certainly didn't improve it. I hung around, knowing no one and feeling very uncomfortable, hoping I would be called upon soon so that I could get my part over with. "This couldn't be a more miserable experience," I noted unhappily as I was walking toward the dais. And then I remembered the assignment. Walking to the podium, I thought "spirit and love," and I felt my posture change and my heart expand. I stood at the podium for a moment, taking in everyone and everything, and began to sing "Danny Boy" from some deep part of me—I just let it go. It was really awesome.
>
> Afterward a man came up to me and said, "When you sang there was so much love in the room. I could feel your spirit." Can you believe that? And later I saw in a video that I was *smiling* throughout "Danny Boy."

Another story of the power of this assignment comes from a violist named Amalia Arnoldt. In 2004, the Berlin Symphony announced that it was holding auditions for the position of leader of the viola section. Amalia knew that up to this point no orchestra in Germany had ever employed a woman as leader, and few had many women players in their ranks at all. So she estimated that her chances were very slim indeed, but she signed up to try out primarily for the experience. Amalia was nervous enough anticipating playing in front of an austere group of male judges who had not yet found a woman to be up to the mark, but then she discovered that her teacher was auditioning for the position as well! This was impossible! Any small hope she still held out for winning the audition dwindled to nothing at the news.

However, Amalia bravely went ahead, and when it was her turn to play she quite fortuitously remembered her time in Ben's interpretation class at the New England Conservatory, and the assignment "Walk with Spirit and Love." As she brought the practice into consciousness, her posture and her attitude changed radically. And as she performed, spirit and love found their way into the music. The result was that in November 2004, the Berlin Symphony, for the first time in its history, seated a woman, Amalia Arnoldt, in a leadership position as first chair. We can imagine that this young woman was highly skilled when she played for those judges, and perhaps she would have won the position on mastery alone, but Amalia herself has no doubt as to what to attribute this outcome: she says it was all due to the simple, wholly transformational practice of "walking with spirit and love."

SPIRIT AND LOVE ON CITY STREETS

I remember a transformational moment that came to me in my early twenties that was foundational for me in inventing this game and did in fact initiate a new stage in my life. I was living in New York City at the time, eight long blocks from the subway that took me to Greenwich Village, where I worked in a therapy center for autistic children. One of those blocks was wholly taken up with a huge construction site that I was bound to pass daily as the only reasonable route to the subway entrance. In those days, young women were a favorite distraction and fair game for the guys on those jobs. Every day I steeled myself to pass through their whistles as though deaf to their detailed observations of the outfit I was wearing and the features they imagined to belong to the body beneath. Sometimes, if I had time, I took a long way around, but not without cost. Having to take a detour made me feel thoroughly victimized.

Then one morning out of the blue I did something entirely different. I didn't plan it, I can say only I was inspired, moved, led to take action with no thought behind it at all. This particular morning I stopped in the middle of the catcalls, turned to the men, and with a broad open smile called out, "How flattering!" Behind their chain-link fence, the attack dogs turned instantly into happy wriggling puppies. "You've made my day," I said, genuinely, because at this point it was true. I remember standing straight and powerful, and the feeling of joy. I talked to the men every day after that, and got to know a little about some of them, how the job suited one, and where another lived. One of them showed me a picture of his kid when I told him I worked with children. I advised them to keep on whistling because it made me feel good.

Walking in this manner, with spirit and love, I never again felt afraid of attention of that sort. For one thing, my response of "thank you, that's a compliment" seemed to establish an instant caring and respect between us, and nobody ever took advantage of me. I find myself walking this way in all kinds of circumstances. When I meet a panhandler who asks me for money I either give him some or I say, "Not today, but good luck." And I look him right in the eye and smile, because the one gift I can always provide is the gift of relationship, and turning away as though he doesn't exist is far worse in my mind than an overt refusal to let him have some of my money.

SPIRIT AND LOVE ON OTHER STREETS

On a trip to Panama with my friend Anne, we spent a night in a mutual friend's apartment in Panama City. It was Good Friday and toward evening the narrow streets turned into flowing rivers of celebrants, dotted with the light of myriad candles. We followed, enthralled; and then on an impulse decided to take an empty side street down to the ocean to catch our first view of the sea in the last light of day.

As soon as we separated from the crowds I had an uneasy feeling. I registered the disparity of means between us, as tourists, and the inhabitants of this part of the city and I encouraged the fearless Anne to walk back up to the square. But it was too late. I suddenly became aware of a man moving swiftly on my left, and I shrank away toward the wall of a building to protect my backpack. He grabbed me around my neck and seemed intent on strangling me, but I registered at once that he was applying far too little force to be able to do real damage. I peeled his hands off my neck, and held his wrists in front of me. He was thin, I noticed. I looked him in the eyes, searching, smiled slowly, and shook my head mouthing "No." He wrenched his hands free and went back to "strangling" me; I took his hands away and smiled "No." We went through this ritual a couple more times, he squeezing my neck, but not too hard, me pulling him off by the wrists, looking deep into his eyes, each time making a bit more of a connection, and eventually he ran away. Meanwhile, Anne was looking for help, but the police, who were situated two blocks away, paid us no attention.

My assailant returned, however, made another attempt, and then ran again. Ultimately I realized that he was trying to get my jewelry—although it was not at all apparent to me during the encounter—because when we got back to the apartment where we were staying, I saw that the necklace I'd forgotten I was wearing had snapped and fallen into my clothes, and that I was holding my watch, the band of which was now broken, in my hand. Curious. How would I have it in my hand? He must have broken the band and taken the watch, and I must have politely taken it back.

The lesson in this story is certainly not to be either sweet or imperious with your attacker. It's more of a discovery. Walking with Spirit and Love brings you into a remarkable state of presence where you can optimally interact with the world before you. I found myself telling this chap very clearly that he wasn't to trespass, at the same time that I was radiating love and spirit. Do you think he came back again because he was curious about this encounter? He took nothing away with him. He even left my backpack with me.

Many have asked after reading such stories, "How do you inspire those around you with spirit and love when they don't seem to be interested or want to do anything themselves?" This is a very widespread concern that stems, I believe, from the almost universal assumption that you have only limited powers, if any, to change other people. It is common wisdom that trying to get people to follow your agenda is a pretty hit-or-miss affair, no matter how intensely you feel it would be for their own good. But in another way of thinking, each of us has ultimate power to change the world, because we have absolute power to rewrite our own story. Walk with Spirit and Love is a new script for you, and as is true for all new scripts, when you take it on you will walk in a different world where everyone in it is altered and changed.

I encourage you to make Walk with Spirit and Love a daily practice. It delivers you from self-concern, heightens your awareness, slows down the rush of time, and gives you joy, just as it does to those around you.

> The thought manifests as the word;
> The word manifests as the deed;
> The deed develops into habit;
> And the habit into character.
>
> So watch the thought and its ways with care
> And let it spring from love
> Born out of concern for all Beings.
> As the shadow follows the body,
> As we think, so we become.
>
> —Anonymous (often attributed to the Buddha from
> *The Dhammapada*)

See What You've Never Seen Before

WHEN MY DAUGHTER, ALEXANDRA, was three years old, I arranged a playdate for her and a preschool friend, Julie, a clever, resourceful little girl. We lived in a rambling house that Julie had visited several times. Previously Julie's mother had delivered her to our front door, but this time it was I who picked the girls up from school, parked in the garage, and walked them up the hill to the back door. Julie came into the house for the first time through the kitchen and stood stock-still, looking around. Then she brightened. "Oh, you've moved," she declared.

When you are three, almost everything you do is new to you. Very few layers, if any, of previous interpretation blanket each novel experience, so you are likely to feel joy and wonder or, in some cases, terror, acutely. Then the mind gets to work, fitting what just happened into a scheme of interpretation that will short-cut for Julie her confused surprise at walking in the back door of our house and seeing the kitchen from a different angle. The story she constructed, "Oh, you've moved," with all its charm would soon be replaced by what the neuroscientists call an "invariant" representation. Pretty soon Julie would probably not even have no-ticed differences of approach to a room, certainly not with such astonishment, because she would have an invariant schema, a pro-totype of "room" altering her perception, and preventing her from seeing so precisely the angles and colors and arrangement of items that led her to conclude she was in a different house altogether.

The brain constructs. Fresh data travels up from the bottom to be perceived and interpreted while already-processed representa-tions travel down from above to help make perception efficient.* When we lock in a childhood story like "I can't be trusted," as did little Sam who pinched the flowers for his mother, it becomes a dominant invariant interpretation that guides and constricts our perception from then on. In general as we get older and have more experience, the conceptual layer thickens and affords us fewer and fewer unadulterated moments. Information becomes less acute, less dense, and therefore less interesting. We begin to believe we have seen everything, and get bored; we are under the illusion that we know everything and head off other people's attempts to present us with anything new.

Wake up!

It's your perception that is dulled, not the infinitely faceted frac-tal world before you. You simply can't see or hear or feel your sur-roundings, inside or out, because of the covering layers of filter; and it's not your fault, it's simply the way it works. While, unbe-knownst to us, our minds are developing in this pattern, the world

---

* Daniel J. Siegel, M.D., *Mindsight: The New Science of Personal Transformation* (New York: Bantam, 2010).

itself is losing none of its luster, its capacity to excite. Just watch any three-year-old.

So here is the next game: See What You've Never Seen Before. Experience something new.

Here's how to set this up:

Throw out a frame that is likely to enhance your chances of seeing something new. As an example, a teacher in Hawaii gave her second-grade students disposable cameras and sent them out one morning to take pictures of evidence of God. The results? Happy, excited children; magnificent, creative photos.

Another framework that will improve your chances of a discovery is to do something you are ordinarily very unlikely to do. I was telling a friend about this game and he confessed that he had just gone on an overnight camping trip with his sons and grandchildren, something he had never done before. It came to him in the middle of the night bright with stars that he deprives himself of great experiences by being so exacting of others and so rule bound. As he recounted this for me, he searched for the word.

"Rigid?" I queried.

"Yes," he said, "rigid." This was not a new thought for many of us who know him, but it was for him. "I never saw it before," he said.

You might try drawing the Atlantic Ocean from memory, then open an atlas and observe the shapes of the oceans as though they are the "figure," not the "ground," as though the oceans are the continents; or simply turn your maps upside down and get used to the new look as right side up.

Psychologist Steven Pinker asserts, "There is no reason to believe that what we see bears any resemblance whatsoever to what is out there." Perhaps you will make that your mantra for your day. If you don't become dizzy with the thought, you may begin to notice coincidences of conversations or become aware of "negative spaces"—the intervals between birdcalls, for instance, or the shapes the sky makes between trees. You might even become seriously curious about the phenomenon that you "know" who it is that is calling when the telephone rings.

And if you aspire to be a traveler into lands that are information-
ally rich and diverse, ask yourself, "How is my spouse or child or
friend different from what I have thought?" and keep looking for
signs of divergence from your tightly held assumptions.

A BRILLIANT DESIGN

In Maine, in the summer, I love to go down to the cove at high tide
and throw myself with determined enthusiasm into the water. People "from away" often refer to the ocean water here as the "icy waters of Maine"—and shiver at the thought. I find swimming in this
water exhilarating and it certainly wakes me up, but my memory of
any particular swim soon fades into a generic "dip in the cove."
That is, until something different happens, as it did a few days ago.
    I stepped into the water above the rock my little granddaughter
sits on to watch her elder brother swim, took a few steps, experienced a hesitation to plunge in, and then plunged right in. Exhal-
ing with a laugh, I swam vigorously to the rocks on the other side
that were lit by the afternoon sun, and when I got quite close I saw
a glint of sunlight on a thread. The face of the rock rises almost
vertically so it is not possible to climb out anywhere near there, but
you can hold on to a spur or protuberance in the wall, which I did
to get a closer look.
    The sun had been shining off spokes of spider silk that formed
an armature of a soon-to-be-woven web. By the time I arrived a
small, quite round spider had built the first two rows of a web that
described a circle greater than a foot in diameter so I had gotten in
pretty much on the ground floor. I watched in disbelief as she relentlessly and dexterously pursued her task of building this elaborate structure. In a series of competent moves, she let out her silk,
catching it up with one of her legs as a knitter would pick up a
stitch, and with other legs, which were all the while scuttling along
on their spherical rounds, she attached each row at even intervals
to the armature. I hung in the water watching her, unaware of the

cold, eager to see this whole process through. As time went on I tried to calculate the revolutions she had made by estimating the number of rows, but I got lost somewhere around fifty.

Wasn't she getting tired? How was she going to end this? She busily performed her skilled and intricate work spinning perfect little ladder rungs that gradually diminished in size until she came to a point one row away from the center. I watched, riveted. Then she took a sidewise step and situated herself elegantly at the hub of her sparkling creation. And sat and waited. I longed to send insects her way, and actually tried to do so, only sinking myself in the effort. Again I had an urge to wait, this time until she had caught her dinner, but now for the first time I began to feel the cold and became aware that hypothermia might be in the offing.

I came back the next day hoping to find the spider, but she and her exquisite handiwork were gone. Sadly, the rock showed no trace of yesterday's dramatic production. Part of the wonder of the experience was the surprising affection that developed in me for the spider and my wistfulness at her departure. I have always said that attention is like light and air and water, it grows whatever it shines upon. Now I have to add that attention creates the ground for love to flower.

My swim the previous day was definitely not a generic one. I saw something miraculous I had never seen before. As I emerged from the water this time I reminded myself to stop and look around. As I did so the cove opened up in slow motion in a cinematic extravaganza, everything seeming to point to a little island straight out to sea. I breathed in the beauty—each rocky edge of coastline, each spruce tree seemed clearer and brighter than it ever had—and I thought, "The inward- and outwardness of this, the interpenetration of heart and world . . . this is what I mean by the Territory Beyond."

Let Go

I RECENTLY OVERHEARD A GOLF pro explaining to some expert players that *letting go* is the primary skill necessary to be a consistently good golfer. The important thing is to let go of trying to manage your shot, to let go of the resistance that occurs when you want to avoid mistakes, and the ignominy and shame that accompanies them. He himself hardly looks at the ball, he said; he is looking ahead, seeing the trajectory of his own swing. He said most people focus on the ball and imagine that golf is about whacking the little thing toward the hole and sinking it, but he claimed that isn't what it's about. The important thing, he says, is the continuous free swing of the club through the impact, as though the ball were incidental.

I'm not a golfer myself, but it seems he is saying that a player can get so focused on doing things right, making the short-term goal, and "looking good" to others that he never develops a great swing, and a great swing seems to be central to being a great golfer. "Letting go" of those things is the key to being a consistently good player: not one who never makes mistakes, but one who is skilled overall.

It's a paradox: developing the skill to let go of worries, to let go of whatever you claim you are right about or feel you deserve recognition for—letting go of fears and prejudices, tension and efforts at avoidance—ironically gives you power in your life, the very thing you were trying to accomplish through evasion and resistance. It's the freedom and power of knowing you can handle any situation with grace, without getting stuck in the middle. Let's call it the power of a continuous free swing.

So here's the game: resist, and let go. Hold on to an opinion passionately, and then drop it. Be obsessive about figuring something out, and then let it go. Be righteously indignant and then release the whole thing. Letting go is an interior action, but an action nonetheless. The action feels like a release, followed by an infusion of pleasure and peace.

Letting go is a very different action from the slump into despair you can experience when you give up because things are too tough. Letting go returns you to the present moment, which you may not realize you have ever left, and gets you back into the flow of things. It does wonders for the people around you.

In 2008 I participated in an a public event in South Africa where I made some serious errors, and in an attempt to save the day I learned to let go of types of resistance that I had no idea I was holding. I remarked to a large audience of South Africans in which each race was fairly represented that in this newly liberated environment, journalists had a fabulous opportunity to tell the stories of everyday heroes that would carry the society forward. The audience erupted in applause. At that time, the Johannesburg newspapers were disproportionately devoting their first four pages to images of violence, and I assumed from the applause that I had read the crowd correctly: people wanted to highlight the stories that illuminated the acts of generosity that abound in their country, rather than rape and murder.

When I returned to my hotel, a member of the press who had attended the talk approached me in anger. "You are advocating positive thinking and censorship of the press," she declared. "If we don't emphasize what is going wrong, South Africa could turn into another Zimbabwe!" I was quite startled by her vehemence, but I realized I had not kept in mind that journalists were likely to have been present at my talk. In a sense I had blamed them for standing in the way of the country's development. Not wanting to face my error, my first impulse was to justify my behavior. I claimed that I was not advocating positive thinking. I told her that I define "positive thinking" as akin to putting frosting over a cake you know is moldy and cheerfully serving it up. Instead, I explained, I was suggesting a possibility approach, where the good and bad are in natural balance.

By defending myself this way, I was as much as saying she was wrong and I was right. She clearly didn't share my alarm that frontloading the newspapers with stories of violence seeded fear and gave the false impression that all of society was on a destructive course. Her view, more informed on the ground, was that waking up the citizenry to the presence of crime and violence was the best route to get these unwanted acts under control.

As we stood face-to-face, I could feel the resistance in both of our bodies. "Letting go" was complicated by my realization that I had done her a bad turn, along with the press in general, and that I had just thrown altogether too many words at her to justify my position. So it went in layers. After a struggle, I first let go of my impulse to convince her of my point, and second I let go of my desire to prove to her that I meant well, and third, I let go of my shame at being so thoughtless. My shame was the thing that was most fundamental, and was keeping me stuck.

When those three steps were completed I looked into her fiery eyes and saw what I hadn't seen earlier: her passion to save South Africa from Zimbabwe's fate. Now I was without any resistance and

I told her I understood the vital nature and magnitude of her mission. It allowed me to smile at her with genuine warmth and I took her hand. I felt a slight yielding on her part, a small release inside the tentative grasp. She looked away. "Thank you," she said very briefly, her eyes cast aside. It seemed to me that we were converted there and then to allies in a great cause, each of us slightly wiser, perhaps, and freer than we were before.

A MATTER OF SCALE

Here is another example. Halfway across the world, Joe and Louise were driving to Zion National Park on their vacation, and along the route got into such a heated discussion that neither could find his or her way back to any kind of harmony. When they reached their destination and checked in to their room, Joe lay down on the bed faced toward the wall, not saying a word, and prepared to take a nap, while Louise put on her hiking shoes and walked out into the park.

Louise walked up and down on the winding hiking path, arguing aloud, making her points one after another, quite oblivious to the scene around her. An hour passed and still she continued to be all wound up with anger and self-righteousness. "Eventually," she said, "I was able to lift my sights just enough to see that I was hiking in an awe-inspiring landscape. Gigantic rocks that had been here forever towered over me—nature at its most magnificent, with no sign of civilization. I thought, 'I'm just me—I'm small in this world,' and this somehow helped me to get my whirling emotions down to size. I commanded myself, 'Louise, let go!' and I discovered that if I pushed myself to do so, I could. I was so surprised. I said to Joe when I got back to the lodge, 'I'm fine now,' and I was, and he was very relieved. The real transformation was how I went from embittered and grievous, and angry and resistant, to being completely fine without ever having to revisit my argument with Joe."

We resist in so many ways. We often resist seeing the obvious—that a lover is unhappy, that an executive director is not suited for the job, that we are being silent too long in a friendship, or that the product we have put so many resources into is about to become obsolete. We resist dealing with our relationships head-on in case we might lose something at the other end. We resist change in all its forms, changing plans, growing older, changing our minds. We resist giving the time to things they call for: lying in bed in the morning, for instance; or hugging our friends for as long as is necessary to make a heart connection; or letting our bodies heal in their own time. We even give the weather grief for being whatever it is on a particular day. We resist stepping into any situation that smacks of the unknown, and we resist the idea of death like crazy. We even resist thinking about good things to come, lest we end up disappointed.

An Unwelcome Interloper

This morning, I was musing about the game of Let Go while relaxing on the couch, having a cup of coffee. Then, with a start, I caught sight of a very large caterpillar hunching along the floor, its body adorned with hairs and spikes. My reaction was extreme. Perhaps because I was so shocked by its intrusion, every part of me felt ill will toward the creature. In addition, I was at a loss for what to do. I'd heard there was an infestation of a new breed of moths that were eating the local deciduous trees, so I didn't want to put it outside, and I was not eager to do away with anything this substantial with my own hands.

Instead, I played the Let Go game with this hairy example of the insect world. From my position on the couch, I willed myself to increase, and keep increasing, my antipathy to it, my horror, my indignation at this invasion, until I felt fully and righteously expressed. Then I breathed in and breathed out, and let my aversion go—I dropped it. In its place, to my surprise, emerged a benign view of the creature, inching along as he is designed to do. And in that space came a realization of how little I know or see or understand, despite my strong reactions. The caterpillar went on his way through my living room, and I have to admit I simply lost track of him.

When you "let go" you are releasing, in one simple motion, the hold that your emotions, assumptions, and opinions have over you. Had the caterpillar really been a danger to me apart from my own story, as for instance the threat that the sounds of someone breaking into my house might indicate, I could have let go of every fear, every bit of resistance, and the sense of danger would have returned. "Letting go" clears you of the agendas you have going from your previous experience, enabling you to contemplate the world before you more fairly as it is. Try it first, perhaps, on something as inconsequential to you as an insect, and then build up to the really entrenched problems you have with your government, your profession, or those you love.

A recent convert to the power of letting go, Adam, tells this story:

> My marriage had been falling apart, slowly, over time. Others had tried to tell me but I was not seeing it. However, one evening a mutual friend came over for dinner and he went on about what a fabulous couch we have. I noticed this as an odd emphasis on our furniture, and then I caught him glancing at Margaret, my wife, and I was hit over the head with the message that they were having an affair. After I confronted her, Margaret moved out, and suddenly we were dealing with children, ages two and four, not as a team, but as single parents.
>
> For a long time I felt altogether too weak to cope well with the situation. My wife and I went to therapy and the therapist told me in private that Margaret was through with the marriage; but I read a book called *Getting the Love You Want* and I felt I now had a way of fixing things if only she

would do the exercises with me that the book recommended. I vowed that I would continue to be patient and hold out for her return.

Months later came the date of a three-day wedding of a relative of Margaret's in Monterey, California, to which we were both invited and for which I had long ago agreed to provide the music. I hadn't communicated with my wife at all in the interim. Part of the program was a dance workshop held in Big Sur, in which both Margaret and I took part. At the end we all collapsed on pillows and I found myself right next to her. I was still very, very angry with her. I wanted to be firm with her that hers was a bad decision and we should work this out, but her hand resting on the pillow caught my eye, and I felt a jolt: she wasn't wearing her wedding ring! I managed to ask her about it. "Oh, yes," she said casually, "I took it off a long time ago."

This was the second monumental shock. I had to get out of that room. I walked directly out into a hallway, not knowing anything about the place, opened a nearby door, and started walking down stone stairs that, it turned out, went hundreds of feet down to the beach. I walked blindly deeper and deeper, deeper into my grief, deeper into the pain, and finally arrived at the water and sat down on a rock, sobbing.

When at last I opened my eyes I saw a group of people — they looked like a family of three generations — wading out of the water, backlit by the sun. They stood in front of a woman who held an urn and they and I watched her tilt it, distributing ashes onto the breeze, the sun behind them, the waves coming in. It was so beautiful! And I had this revelation that this is exactly the way the world is, the waves sprinkled with ashes, coming and going, now here, now no longer. I noticed that a weight had lifted and my grief and pain had completely disappeared and I was smiling! I had let go. In absolute calm I stood up and remembered that I was about to play Bach for the marriage of a couple I adored, with people I love. I was so happy, so joyous! Things had been so ugly and now life was all so beautiful.

Before this moment I hadn't been able to be present, I was insisting on correcting the past; after all I *knew* how to save our marriage, and my right answer was tightly knitted into the fabric of my suffering. Suddenly all that self-righteousness that I had been holding on to, all that obsessive looking for reasons, seemed irrelevant. I had woken up to the world as it was now, and it was stunningly beautiful.

REALITY: A HEALING GRACE

Sometimes a major release is forced upon you, often when the evidence for a different reality from the one you are holding so tightly becomes overwhelmingly compelling—the sight of a naked ring finger, for instance, or perhaps a telephone conversation overheard whose meaning cannot be denied. When you release your resistance and let the truth be what it is, you are never quite the same again. However, that may not be the end of it. You may find there are other sticky places, little adhesions over the same issue, and you may have to let go again. No matter. If this happens just be sure you don't tell yourself the story that you haven't grown at all. Remember, life is moving along at just the right pace, and if you stay with that rhythm and don't put on the brakes, things will evolve and you will heal. Keep letting go.

Get in Tune

"No room! No room!" they cried out when they saw Alice coming.

"There's PLENTY of room!" said Alice indignantly, and she sat down in a large armchair at one end of the table.

"Have some wine," the March Hare said in an encouraging tone.

Alice looked all round the table, but there was nothing on it but tea. "I don't see any wine," she remarked.

"There isn't any," said the March Hare.

"Then it wasn't very civil of you to offer it," said Alice angrily.

"It wasn't very civil of you to sit down without being invited," said the March Hare.

"I didn't know it was YOUR table," said Alice; "it's laid for a great many more than three."

"Your hair wants cutting," said the Hatter.

      LEWIS CARROLL, ALICE'S ADVENTURES IN WONDERLAND

P OOR ALICE TRIES BUT can't get into a conversation that makes any sense to her—she just isn't on the Mad Hatter's wavelength. The thing to notice, though, is how persistent she is in her efforts. Alice is doing what all of Nature does to get in tune, overshooting and undershooting, always approaching but never quite reaching pure harmony. They say that the universe would cease to exist were it to find complete equilibrium. But there is no danger of that—just hark back to your last misunderstanding, or better yet, turn on the news.

So to embark on the exploration "Get in Tune," open yourself to the idea of a complex universe, pulsing and vibrating, that is striving to attune with you. Imagine that everyone you meet desires to be in tune with you, as does everything else under the sun. It's not personal; it's what wants to happen. To attune yourself, pay attention to broad patterns—movement in the tops of the trees out your window, people's paths crisscrossing one another on the busy street below, clouds piling high in the sky, as well as conversations taking place around you at tables in a restaurant. Notice how these patterns relate to *you*. Listen carefully to birdcalls as though they involve *you*. *Notice how things are joined in motion—including you*. Look around for connections everywhere.

One summer in the process of writing *The Art of Possibility* I set up a tent on land I eventually built on and lived by myself in this arrangement for six weeks. I interacted with other people once a week when I went to town for supplies, and in between those visits I stayed by myself on the land, running my computer off a car battery charger. I loved living in the tent. It gave me the solitude I needed for the daunting task of coming up with something from nothing, while filling my nature-thirsty spirit to the brim. Besides, the isolation afforded me, in a very minor version of Monty Roberts's sojourn with the mustangs, an unusual opportunity to get a different perspective on what we take for granted as human nature.

I soon realized my new perspective: I was relating more intimately to trees, tides, birds, and one raccoon, my night visitor, than to my own species. It wasn't long before I noticed that some kind of shift had taken place in me. I saw it first when I inadvertently snapped a dry branch off a spruce tree, felt a disturbance through my body, and heard myself saying, "Sorry."

The biggest revelation came on one of my trips to the grocery store in town, ten miles away. At the store I put the items I needed into a cart, and stepped into line behind a woman who was a stranger to me. Then alongside her, I unloaded the groceries from *her* cart onto the checkout counter. I wasn't helping her: I just hadn't identified those groceries in her cart as hers, and these in my cart as mine. In a sense, I had lost my "normal" boundaries. I would have taken out my wallet to pay for hers if she hadn't got there first. It must have seemed quite out-of-the-ordinary to her because I remember she thanked me rather profusely, which struck me as very strange, and when she was leaving she turned back and she asked me where I lived (!) and if I needed a lift.

What I make of all this is that I must have come into an alternate kind of attunement with the world. I was on my way to losing any sense of hierarchy of importance, or rights of possession, qualities that were not relevant to my forest existence. I lived through crackling lightning, and a windstorm that took the whole tent down, and gorgeous days and nights, and I often went alone in a kayak onto the ocean under the moon. I felt safe as could be. At the end of the summer I came indoors to take care of a friend's dog while she was away, and I couldn't bear it. So the dog and I relocated to the tent and we spent an extra week there until the weather turned too cold to continue.

As the horse whisperer Monty Roberts demonstrated, an isolated wild horse will quickly attune to a receptive human being if there is no other living creature around. Communal mammals, in the absence of their group, will seek to align with any other species that is present, as I did within a few days with the forest and its occupants.

Cosmic Expressions

It's hard to remember that nothing is static. There are no closed systems, anywhere, no matter how convenient it is for us to think there are. Everything changes everything else. My brain was changed in the forest, and Monty Roberts's brain was changed when he embedded with the wild horses in the high desert of Nevada. But that's not all: the molecules of the horses changed in contact with the horse whisperer, and the forest, the birds, the raccoon, and of course the dog were altered by my presence, as well. Thomas Lewis, Fari Amini, and Richard Lannon, neuroscientists and authors of A General Theory of Love, give us a scientific, as well as poetic, point of view on this process:

> The evolution of the limbic brain a hundred million years ago created animals with luminescent powers of emotionality and relatedness, their nervous systems designed to intertwine and support each other like supple strands of a vine.*

How lovingly Nature moves to resolve states of dissonance into states of resonance. Regrettably, the opportunities for falling out of attunement in our demanding lives are far greater than the chances that we will find ourselves in flow all the way around. When the lawn mower breaks down because you forgot where that rock was, and the part you ordered for your car doesn't fit, and your child doesn't get into the school you wanted him to go to, it becomes difficult not to wonder what is wrong with you—or everyone else. But this is a feature of the rhythm of life in the universe. A meteorite can put a crimp in the day of a small planet, just as a tropical storm can send an ecosystem into disarray. It's the ocean's destiny and the planet's to bring itself into order; let's make it ours to tell a

---

* Thomas Lewis, Fari Amini, and Richard Lannon, A General Theory of Love (New York: Random House, 2000), 91.

story of our day that brings us in tune with life's ongoing process of restoration, and to offer wisdom for others to share. I mean, by this, the kind of wisdom that recognizes that we, as well as the bird, the stone, and the star, are all in it together.

If we are out of sorts for a while it might even make sense to get into a habit of apologizing for having allowed the dissonance to go on, whether or not we know how to fix it. It is a step, anyway, and it is of course different from taking the blame, or sacrificing our own contribution to agree with the people we're with. It's even further from an attempt to dominate the situation so that people fall into line. As the knowledgeable kids of Remington Street demonstrated when playing Double Dutch, if you are outside the rhythm, stop, watch, wait, breathe, and then get back into the flow.

A PRACTICE

On a retreat with the enlightened leadership team of a diamond mining company in South Africa, Trans Hex, the seven men and I came up with a procedure to help people attune to one another when a dispute throws them off-track. It was based in the conviction that people as their infinite selves want to come to agreement, but are sometimes held back by their walking story—their overall conception of reality—and/or by the agendas of their child parts. The process allowed a time for letting go of intensity, the loosening of the grip of a story, and a new start. It consisted of three steps. The first was "STOP! Say Nothing and Breathe." Anyone in the group was authorized to call for an instant cessation of turmoil. The second was "Go to the Videotape," and what we meant by that was "Describe what happened that became a problem for you as you would see it on a videotape, without added interpretation, so that everyone present could agree on the facts." For instance, "the videotape" might show the CFO saying, "I meant to get you the figures today, but I haven't finished them," and the CEO saying, "You've had plenty of time, I don't think you understand the importance of this," and slamming his fist on the table. What it wouldn't include would be abstractions like "Arthur was being unfair" or "Don was being manipulative," because neither fairness nor manipulation would ever leave an image on a photographic plate. When there was consensus on exactly what happened as seen on film, we went to step three: "Make a Request." For example: "Will you get me the figures by noon tomorrow?" or "Will you listen to what held up the process for me?" Each person was free to accept or decline the request or make a counteroffer. So the process looks like this:

1. STOP! Say nothing and breathe—it is agreed that anyone in the group can call for a Stop!

2. Revisit the problem scene as though on videotape, until all can see and agree on what happened, devoid of interpretation.

3. Make a request.

Now six years later, Trans Hex is still operating by the principles we developed then. When they enter a new region to work a mine, it is their policy to start planning for restoring the land and supporting cottage industries so that the local people will enjoy a sustainable lifestyle when Trans Hex leaves the area. They build agriculture and small businesses and strive to preserve the beauty of the landscape and put the earth back as they found it. And they added a diamond cutting and polishing unit to their repertoire in order to provide more jobs for the local people. This company did the internal work that has kept them well in tune with their own people and able to attune with the environments they enter and the people in them. In a highly unusual move, the diverse leadership team took themselves off-line for four days and dug deep into their own histories, many of which were very fraught and complicated by the transition from an apartheid society. They connected with one another over the moving personal stories of their early lives, some extremely traumatic, when few of them shared a similar status, but all shared a desire for a unified country. They adopted the principles of possibility thinking, and they created a new image for themselves as conscious contributors to humanity rather than simply guardians of their shareholders' wealth. The process brought these seven leaders into profound resonance. Interestingly, they were the only diamond mining company in South Africa that came out cash positive the following year, or so they tell me.

Many organizations strive for this kind of attunement, but few attain it as Trans Hex did at that time. The best of them spend months working on their vision, mission, and value statements, making an effort to involve representatives from all levels of the company. What kind of results do they produce? Their results are often remarkably similar to those of every other conscientious organization. Most companies profess to believe, for example, in teamwork, integrity, passion, and transparency, and they name the customer as their focus. Most of them discover in their visioning process exactly the qualities universally aspired to in human spiritual development. Why, then, in contrast to Trans Hex, are their beautifully crafted statements so easily forgotten and rendered ineffective by those who matter most in carrying them out?

To poor Alice, this seems like more of the Mad Hatter's crazy world that she simply can't get in tune with. That may be because there is a piece of the equation missing! Most companies put all their attention on the expansive side, the world out there and their mission in regard to it. They leave out completely the inner work of the employees as instruments of its expression. So no matter that the organization spent thousands on developing a vision or a statement of purpose, and no matter that the employees post it on the walls in their office and receive daily e-mails from management as a reminder and are able to recite it on cue. Unless the CEO is talking about his own struggle to maintain integrity or passion in his daily life, or the management team is discussing the waning of transparency in their personal relationships, the polished mission and value statements will have no resonance with the people. How many leaders do you know who are paying attention to the contractive side and looking deeply into themselves as living examples of their mission? And how many companies offer their employees an ongoing structure, such as the games, to do the same? To run a company where there is no enduring evolution toward attunement between the mission and values on the one hand and the personal development of the employees on the other is like trying to blow up a balloon without using your lungs. Lip service won't do it.

When a group gets into resonance it is likely that it can quadruple the output that a leader can accomplish by orders alone, and when you have an attuned team there is generally no need to drive people or ride herd on their projects. For example, when the Boston Philharmonic Youth Orchestra went on tour their very first year to Holland, they brought along only 4 chaperones for 120 young people, ages twelve to twenty-one, in the conviction that the orchestra had become a mature, responsible body over the months of rehearsals, the assignments and games, and their ongoing dialogue with the conductor through their weekly writing assignments. It's natural for people to align, especially when they are given the time and space to examine their outdated assumptions, such as that teenagers are irresponsible, or adults are all control freaks, and grow beyond them.

At the midpoint of the tour, the kids, the chaperones, and the three-person staff came together in a meeting that mimicked the feedback loop process of an orchestra tuning. The entire discussion was held in the form of requests, from all sides. "Will you arrange it so we have more time to warm up?" for example, or "Will you pack your bags and leave them in the lobby the night before for an early start?" In response to any question, "yes" or "no" was a valid answer; if "no," people agreed to make a counteroffer or request. They covered an enormous amount of ground in the meeting and the group ended up perfectly in tune. With this kind of attunement a leader can focus on special events—things that wouldn't happen otherwise—and can then infuse the organization with energy and direction that goes beyond what players, workers, or staff can do on their own, rather than expend resources on compliance. This is where leadership and management part company and the organization has the possibility of entering the Territory Beyond.

Nature has helpers everywhere to bring the cacophonous vibrations of the universe into harmony, because everything is designed to work with her, sharing information in an infinite feedback loop of output and reception, expansion and contraction, as at every point adjustments are made. Dolphins, for instance, are some of Nature's most skilled ambassadors. The sound pattern they use to orient themselves, echolocation, is soothing to human brain wave patterns and brings them into coherence. When children, especially autistic children, swim with dolphins and are immersed in a field of dolphin sounds, their attention span often lengthens, their motor skills improve, and they become more coordinated.

It appears that some of what dolphins can do with sound, you can do with your brain and heart, as research at the Kavli Institute for Systems Neuroscience in Trondheim, Norway, has shown us. When people are attuned to one another, their energy is amplified, and their cells vibrate together.

The late Dr. Masaru Emoto is by now well known in alternative circles for his findings about the effect of music and human consciousness on water crystals, work that is edging toward wider acceptance. He drew hundreds of samples of water at intervals, over time, from different sources worldwide, from the purest mountain streams to the most chemically polluted lakes, and he froze the water and then brought it into crystalline form. He also subjected the different samples to an array of positive and negative words and to music from classical to heavy metal in an attempt to find out what effect human activity and human consciousness might have on the water.

As his laboratory raised the temperature of the specimens of frozen water, crystals formed into distinct and surprising shapes. The water from the pure streams grew balanced symmetrical crystals, and the polluted water produced dark, ugly, shapeless material. The water samples that were exposed to loving words formed beautiful and striking crystalline structures, and those exposed to words of hate and anger showed up in unattractive, formless shapes, in some cases with no discernible geometry.

He experimented with the music of the Beatles, "Amazing Grace," "Edelweiss," and classical music, all of which produced gorgeous crystals that differed markedly with each composer. Responding to Bach, the water actually grew variations on a theme! But frozen water came up disorganized and darkened in the presence of music that lay on the spectrum of heavy metal and alternative rock. Dr. Emoto's experiments have been repeated many times with the same range of results, and are sufficient proof to some that human emotions affect matter.

If we can alter, by loving, appreciative thoughts, the structure of the material that makes up nearly 60 percent of our bodies, might we not do good things for ourselves and others by consistently producing those thoughts? Dr. Emoto discovered that the words "thank you" produced exceptional shapes, but the words "love and gratitude" had the strongest effect on H_2O, resulting in the most unequivocally clear and beautiful crystals of all.

Opportunities for getting in tune exist wherever we turn if we look for them. If you want to have an extraordinary experience of attunement, swim with a dolphin, paste words of love and gratitude on your water bottle, venture into the wilderness for a week or two, or align the inside and the outside of people in your company with your shared purpose, paying close attention to what's happening inside you as well. Look all around for connections on every scale and send love and appreciation along those shimmering threads.

Epilogue

As those children who had a time-share with the cars on Remington Street understood, life is a cooperative venture. It takes awareness, rhythm, coordination, and joie de vivre to live it fully. Through these pages we have increased our awareness of two vast interpenetrated arenas of human experience. One is the ecology of internal life, and the second is the world we relate to outside our skin.

Looking inward, we brought a kindness and light to those deeply emotional children of ours, locked away below our consciousness, whose growth had been arrested in midflight. We weren't even aware of their presence, waiting there for us to see and hear them and give them proper care. Nor did we realize what a difference it would make to us to welcome them fully grown—the risk takers, the lovers, the skilled and the competent—into partnership with us as life goes forward.

In order to best help them we named ourselves as a field, a field of awareness, and gave ourselves a place to stand outside the commotion of their voices. Then we could attend to helping them

242

grow, in the right rhythm, without prejudice. We learned that emotions don't heal all at once, but at a slower pace than thoughts, and only in the medium of love.

Then the brilliant world of stories opened up: child stories, safety patterns, adult stories, walking stories, and luminous new stories initiating new patterns, with instructions on how to write them. We realized that when we upgraded those child stories and created wholeness, we could provide the conditions for the adult in other people to emerge. How different from trying to fix them or combat them!

Looking outward, we began to expand the frame of our view to be better predictors of the direction of life on the move, as we seek to get into the game. It's a rhythm thing. If you get it right, a little blast of energy in a small hut in Puebla, or in a business meeting in Japan, can initiate a significant evolution that—who knows?—could become a new fractal pattern. And it's all because you were in tune with the possibility of that change that was waiting in the wings.

Next we allowed our minds to be stretched and pulled to accommodate what we might ordinarily have made no time for in our everyday lives. We visualized the mysterious migratory paths of butterflies and imagined that rocks are conscious and that trees protect one another by sending messages to the very edges of the forest. We gave consideration to tales that one mind has an effect on another across distances, and that water responds to words of love and gratitude. We were introduced to the astonishing phenomenon of fractal patterns lying right under our noses, and remembering the butterflies, we began to appreciate the complexity with which Nature evolves, integrating random occurrences into her order as life-forms develop whatever capacities they need to thrive.

Our view of the world began to shift away from seeing things as solid matter in closed systems—people as identities, and things as inanimate—and opened up to the startling fields of energy around us. We began to get a feel for Nature and her infinite regenerative and creative capacities and started to attune to them. We saw that what our heart puts out is the source of relatedness and can make a difference to the ongoing life of the planet, its survival and vitality.

Many times along the way we made mini-adjustments to the story of who we are: a "field," "not the doer," "a channel for information." We made further adjustments on the startling realization that the human race and Nature are in a perilous arrangement. Having seen that Nature is working for us and we are working for ourselves, we created a new story as "partners in evolution."

And with that new "identity" we agreed to take on a role of extraordinary responsibility, as cocreators and coevolvers with Nature herself, with equally extraordinary rewards: deep connections among ourselves and synergy everywhere, spectacular beauty, unbounded vitality, and the accompaniment of galactic support wherever we go. Well, not quite. We'll have the support as long as we stay aware of the rhythms, make course corrections when we are off-track, and choose a path that is waiting to open up.

To remind us of the track, we now have infinite games to play. In an instant we can have all the time in the world, and with a shift of posture we can spread spirit and love wherever we go. The inside and the outside of us are enriched by our openness to seeing the world anew. And when we decline to be caught by old issues and we let them go, we find ourselves in tune and able to sense the music of all creation.

I feel enormously grateful that you, the reader, have traveled this far, which has landed you, with me, somewhere in the middle of the paradox that life is. We have a long way to go, you and I, along our path into resonance with everything under the sun. Be forewarned that even as we enjoy such a moment, we will probably have to circle back, clear some more assumptions, and raise our energy to go forward again. However, as I'm sure you will remind me, in the Territory Beyond where we dwell, there is, fortunately, all the time in the world for the journey.

Acknowledgments

First I want to thank and acknowledge those who have actually been in the trenches with me over this book. Kathryn Court and Lindsey Schwoeri at Penguin Random House have been dream editors, inspiring, smart, flexible, and above all patient, with expert backup from Ike Williams, agent extraordinaire. I was also immensely helped and supported by the editorial skills of Jenna Land Free of Girl Friday Productions who was not only swift and able but was lighthearted and encouraging when I was down in the dumps, and tough as tacks when she thought I was on the wrong track.

My deep appreciation goes to my family and close friends, who changed their plans so often over the last few years to accommodate my need to isolate myself to get the work done. I can't say enough about how vitally important their kindness, understanding, and forgiveness were to me. I am painfully aware that every action has its consequences, and while I do not regret all that it took me to produce *Pathways*, I am sorry for every moment I missed with the people I love.

The writing of *Pathways* was as much a journey of growth and transformation for me as I intend it to be for the reader. I want to thank the brilliant people who worked with me in my effort to change my own patterns, and those patient souls who altered my view of the body, and the generous people who introduced me to new concepts that stretched my mind, all in the essential context of love. Also to the many of you who provided stories, turned me on to new information, read chapters, and went beyond the call of duty in so many other ways to help me, I am very, very grateful.

Recommended Reading

Philosophy

Bateson, Gregory. *Mind and Nature: A Necessary Unity*. Cresskill, NJ: Hampton Press, Inc., and The Institute for Intercultural Studies, 2002.

——. *Steps to an Ecology of Mind: Collected Essays in Anthropology, Psychiatry, Evolution, and Epistemology*. 1st ed. Chicago: The University of Chicago Press, 2000.

Carse, James. *Finite and Infinite Games: A Vision of Life as Play and Possibility*. New York: Free Press, 1986.

Frankl, Viktor E. *The Will to Meaning: Foundations and Applications of Logotherapy*. New York: Meridian, 1988.

Haidt, Jonathan. *The Happiness Hypothesis: Finding Modern Truth in Ancient Wisdom*. New York: Basic Books, 2006.

Kuhn, Thomas. *The Structure of Scientific Revolutions*. 4th ed. Chicago: University of Chicago Press, 2012.

Neuroscience and Attachment Theory

Buczynski, Ruth. "New Brain Science," Webinar Series, National Institute for the Clinical Application of Behavioral Medicine, http://www.nicabm.com/nicabmblog/.

Doidge, Norman. *The Brain That Changes Itself: Stories of Personal Triumph from the Frontiers of Brain Science*. New York: Penguin Books, 2007.

Eagleman, David. *Incognito: The Secret Lives of the Brain*. New York: Vintage, 2012.

Lewis, Thomas, Fari Armini, and Richard Lannon. *A General Theory of Love*. New York: Random House, 2000.

Ogden, Pat, and Janina Fisher. *Sensorimotor Psychotherapy: Interventions for Trauma and Attachment*. New York: W. W. Norton, 2015.

Siegel, Daniel. *The Developing Mind: How Relationships and the Brain Interact to Shape Who We Are*. New York: The Guilford Press, 1999.

——. *Mindsight: The New Science of Personal Transformation*. New York: Bantam Books, 2010.

Music

Sacks, Oliver. *Musicophilia: Tales of Music and the Brain*. Rev. ed. New York: Vintage Books, 2008.

Wong, Lisa, with Robert Viagas. *Scales to Scalpels: Doctors Who Practice the Healing Arts of Music and Medicine*. New York: Pegasus Books, 2012.

Business

Kegan, Robert, and Lisa Laskow Lahey. *Immunity to Change: How to Overcome It and Unlock the Potential in Yourself and Your Organiza-*

tion (Leadership for the Common Good). Cambridge, MA: Harvard Business Review Press, 2009.

Senge, Peter M., Otto C. Scharmer, Joseph Jaworski, and Betty Sue Flowers. *Presence: An Exploration of Profound Change in People, Organizations, and Society*. New York: Crown Business, 2005.

Wheatley, Meg. "The Unplanned Organization: Learning from Nature's Emergent Creativity." *Noetic Sciences Review* 37 (Spring 1996).

Physics

Haramein, Nassim. The Resonance Project. http://resonance.is.

Pagels, Heinz R. *The Cosmic Code: Quantum Physics as the Language of Nature*. New York: Simon & Schuster, 1982.

Science Daily Staff. "Golden Ratio Discovered in Quantum World: Hidden Symmetry Observed for the First Time in Solid State Matter." *Science Daily*, January 7, 2010. http://www.sciencedaily .com/releases/2010/01/100107143909.htm.

Talbot, Michael. *The Holographic Universe*. New York: HarperCollins, 1991.

The Natural Sciences

Benyus, Janine M. *Biomimicry: Innovation Inspired by Nature*. New York: William Morrow and Company, Inc., 1997.

Goodall, Jane, with Gail Hudson. *Seeds of Hope: Wisdom and Wonder from the World of Plants*. New York: Grand Central Publishing, 2014.

Thomas, Lewis. *Lives of a Cell: Notes of a Biology Watcher*. New York: Penguin Books, 1978.

Marais, Eugene. *The Soul of the White Ant*. Review Press, 2009.

NOVA. *Fractals: Hunting the Hidden Dimension*. PBS Home Video, 2009.

Roberts, Monty. *The Man Who Listens to Horses: The Story of a Real-Life Horse Whisperer*. New York: Ballantine Books, 2008.

Sheldrake, Rupert. *Dogs That Know When Their Owners Are Coming Home and Other Unexplained Powers of Animals* (Kindle Edition). New York: Three Rivers Press, 2011.

Environment

Friedman, Thomas L. "The Inflection is Near?" The Opinion Pages. *New York Times*, March 7, 2009. http://www.nytimes.com/2009/03/08/opinion/08friedman.html.

Gilding, Paul. *The Great Disruption: Why the Climate Crisis Will Bring On the End of Shopping and the Birth of a New World*. New York: Bloomsbury Press, 2011.

Hawken, Paul. *Blessed Unrest: How the Largest Movement in the World Came into Being and Why No One Saw It Coming*. New York: Viking, 2007.

Smith, Daniel B. "Is There an Ecological Unconscious?" *The New York Times Magazine*, January 27, 2010.

Anthropology

Almond, Steve. "Economic Lessons from the Playground." Opinion. *Boston Globe*, November 16, 2009.

Campbell, Joseph, with Bill Moyers. *The Power of Myth*. New York: Anchor Books, 1991.

Hartmann, Thom. *The Last Hours of Ancient Sunlight: Waking Up to Personal and Global Transformation*. New York: Three Rivers Press, 2000.

Lopez, Barry. *Arctic Dreams*. New York: Vintage, 2001.

Consciousness

HeartMath Institute. https://www.heartmath.org.

Martin, Stephan. *Cosmic Conversations: Dialogues on the Nature of the Universe and the Search for Reality*. Wayne, NJ: New Page Books, 2009.

Mitchell, Edgar D., and Robert Staretz. "The Quantum Hologram And the Nature of Consciousness." *Journal of Cosmology* 14 (2011).

Norretranders, Tor. *The User Illusion: Cutting Consciousness Down to Size*. Penguin Books, 1999.

Extraordinary Experience

Alexander, Eben. *Proof of Heaven: A Neurosurgeon's Journey into the Afterlife*. New York: Simon & Schuster, 2012.

Emoto, Masaru. *The Hidden Messages in Water*. Hillsboro, OR: Beyond Words, 2004.

Mayer, Elizabeth Lloyd. *Extraordinary Knowing: Science, Skepticism, and the Inexplicable Powers of the Human Mind*. New York: Bantam Dell, 2007.